THE HIDDEN SECRETS ABOUT YOU

A Short Guide for a Curious Girl to Find Happiness in Daily Life

Nataly Tzertzivadze

Copyright © 2021 Nataly Tzertzivadze.

All rights reserved. No part of this book may be used or reproduced by any means, graphic, electronic, or mechanical, including photocopying, recording, taping or by any information storage retrieval system without the written permission of the author except in the case of brief quotations embodied in critical articles and reviews.

Balboa Press books may be ordered through booksellers or by contacting:

Balboa Press
A Division of Hay House
1663 Liberty Drive
Bloomington, IN 47403
www.balboapress.com
844-682-1282

Because of the dynamic nature of the Internet, any web addresses or links contained in this book may have changed since publication and may no longer be valid. The views expressed in this work are solely those of the author and do not necessarily reflect the views of the publisher, and the publisher hereby disclaims any responsibility for them.

Any people depicted in stock imagery provided by Getty Images are models,
and such images are being used for illustrative purposes only.
Certain stock imagery © Getty Images.

Cover design and typesetting Cutting-edge-studio.com

ISBN: 978-1-9822-6657-8 (sc)
ISBN: 978-1-9822-6658-5 (e)

Library of Congress Control Number: 2021906664

Print information available on the last page.

Balboa Press rev. date: 04/01/2021

CONTENTS

Foreword v

   1   The Laws of the Universe 1

   2   What is God's Design? 17

   3   The Greatness in Small and Details of the Great 32

   4   If youth knew and old age could 41

   5   The Rule Of The Pickled Cucumber 60

   6   The long path to YOURSELF 66

   7   Good morning, God. Today I became a Woman 80

   8   Wow, Corona is here! 89

   9   All that Lola wants 101

Acknowledgements 107

FOREWORD

When I reflect on my life, I, like everyone else, tend to be positive and try to remember only the good things that happened. However, like everyone else, I also have an endless list of mistakes. These mistakes were usually related to a lack of knowledge, lack of life experience, or lack of support at the right moment. Looking back at my entire adolescence, I can now say that it was a long nightmare full of feelings of loneliness, fears, and resentment. I made simple mistakes so many times, just because of a lack of simple life-related knowledge.

We all know what I am talking about, and to be clear, I will tell you many enlightening stories.

How many times do we say to ourselves, "Such a pity! I didn't know that"? Some of our mistakes we can fix, but many of them are irreversible. It is too late at that time though, especially if life-threatening damage has already been done.

I decided to write this book for girls aged between sixteen and nineteen years so that they do not make the same mistakes. Girls this age are so young, so inexperienced, and so unfamiliar with this world. They need our protection, guidance and directions, especially when exposed to the influences of today's environment which emphasises low cultural standards and the poor protection of women. When in effect, young women at this age must be treated as priceless treasures--**with love and endless support**.

Based on a range of material created by David Cottrell, Eric Harvey, Bruce Lipton, and many other mentors of mine, this book covers numerous vital topics relevant to girls aged between sixteen and nineteen years. I use very simple language and real-life examples and talk to our girls like their grandma would talk to them: with endless pride, love, and respect. And as you'll tell from reading this book, I also genuinely worry about them with all my heart.

I will share with them how to maintain their mental and physical health, and how to become successful, self-confident women—women that knows how to transfer their lives into wonderful journeys full of joy and pleasure for not just their own needs but also those of the people around them.

This book, and the others in this series, are dedicated to young women who care about their future. This book is also dedicated to their guardians or close others who care about what happens to their dear girls in everyday life. This book is not for those who believe that life is about begging for undeserved gifts, or for those who are using other people to achieve their goals. This book will not help such immature souls, although, I will pray for them and ask the universe to give them the knowledge and strength to develop their insight.

And, for those girls who have started asking themselves every day, "I wonder why this happened to me today?"--to such smart people, I want to say, "Congratulations! You are great. You are future goddesses!" Because in this book, my goal is to help you to become not only healthy, kind, and omnipotent, but merciful, knowledgeable (you can even say wise), as well as patient with the flaws and stupidities of others. Our conversation in this book will be exciting and straightforward. I promise.

We will cover many topics. In this book, we will talk about the laws of the universe. Specifically, about the universal rules of life which are the same for everyone—for huge animals, and microscopic living organisms, for stars and angels, for fairies, and for everything else that lives in the universe. We will talk about the mighty power of a woman. We will talk about simple strategies we can use to work with our energies. We will talk about how our physical body is structured, and I will explain the deep connection we hold between our organs as well as the wisdom and beauty of a female body.

And most importantly, I will provide simple and easy tips on how to keep a woman's body healthy and forever young and attractive. Following these tips will avoid old age, illnesses, or unhealthy habits making the reader worthy of being called a "True Goddess," an empress, and a great lady of her life.

Yours,

Mama Nata.

THE LAWS OF THE UNIVERSE

There are many laws of the universe, and all of them will affect and control your life. It is valuable to know the most important of these laws, which are:

1. **The law of giving and receiving**
2. **The law of action and reaction**
3. **The law of cause and effect**
4. **The law of internal preparedness**
5. **The law of universal wisdom**
6. **The law of constant movement and transition**
7. **The law of free choice**

From an early age, these laws will help you to go through life smoothly. They will protect you from committing unnecessary, reckless mistakes that will make you feel ashamed in the future. Trust me, my sunshine, there is nothing worse than wishing to change mistakes that cannot be fixed.

We have discussed each of these in depth below.

1. THE LAW OF GIVING AND RECEIVING

The first law is the law of giving and receiving. It can be explained like this: Before you ask the world for something for yourself, first of all, give the world around you a piece of yourself via your blessings or your time. This is a simple and wise law, and as I mentioned earlier, all my stories in this book are either from my life or from the experience of other people that I know, so here, we will begin with a story about a doctor that I once worked with.

> *One boy's mother got sick. Her stomach ached. She began to vomit, lose weight, and was diagnosed with liver cancer. The family tried all kinds of treatments. The treatment courses were massive and long.*
>
> *But nothing was helping, and his mother was fading before his eyes. The boy loved his mother very much and wanted to help her. But he didn't know how. And then one day, he suddenly knew what he had to do. It was as if someone from heaven had told him(please pay attention for what I just said: " Someone from heaven had told him").*
>
> *He raised his eyes to the sun and said with all his heart and the full desire to fulfil his promise, "Lord, please leave my mother on earth, alive and healthy. And I promise you that when I grow up, I will become a doctor, and I will help sick people for the rest of my life. The next morning his mother suddenly asked for food; her recovery was an inexplicable miracle. But the boy knew what the matter had been, and he subsequently grew up and became a famous oncologist —a doctor who treats cancer patients. True to his promise, he saved thousands and thousands of lives and his mother lived another twenty years. In the end, she died not from her illness, but when her time to go had come.*

Many nations call this law "the law of ten." It refers to where you found a hundred, now give ten to the others in need.

Girls, the message here is that if you want to have real success in your life, **be a giving person.**

Give warm words and smiles. Thank the world for all that is beautiful. Share your breakfast with someone who does not have such a breakfast. Share knowledge and support with those in need. Mentally, before you eat your breakfast in the morning, tell the universe, "I want all the children and all the animals on earth to have a delicious breakfast." Every morning, mentally wish this world abundance and joy. These are your first steps towards becoming a Goddess.

2. THE LAW OF ACTION AND REACTION

The second law is the law of action and reaction, or the law of continuous changes. For example: after the night comes the day; after the rain comes out the sun; life is replaced by death; summer changes into winter; healthy may become diseased, and so on. We should always remember that nature has a tendency to constantly make modifications, and the same thing happens to our lives. Our body processes have periodicity and adversity, we simply learn to take these changes calmly and wisely.

Being aware of this law will help you become sturdy and patient. If you are undeservedly offended or you are ill, be prepared for the black and white stripes in your life and remind yourself, "I'm not upset, because this will not always be so." And when everything is awesome, remind yourself that this will not always be so either. Because when we enjoy something, and everything is going great, we must remember that we shouldn't be upset when a change comes into our lives.

The great and wise King Solomon had a ring. When he was angry, he took off this ring and read the inner inscription which said, "And this will pass too."

Be wise, my Goddesses.

3. THE LAW OF CAUSE AND EFFECT

The third law is the law of cause and effect. In India, this is called the law of Karma. My grandmother always used to say to me, "What you plant is what will grow and give you the harvest." This is a fundamental law, but many adults do not understand what it means. Therefore, you must understand this law as soon as possible—for from deliberately wrong actions a reckoning will come, and for good deeds, be sure, the universe will thank you.

Listen to my story:

> *There was a very famous surgeon who could treat a sporadic disease. He performed a very complicated, long surgery which lasted eight hours. During that time, he cut out the diseased organ and created a new one in the human body. Thanks to his work, his patient was able to live for another seven to ten years.*
> *But there was trouble. This surgeon loved money more than anything in the world(what a sin!). Since this operation was costly, and no one else knew how to undertake this type of procedure, he became richer not by the day but by the hours. He did not allow any other doctor to be admitted into the operating room during the operation; he would only accept one other person in the office at a time, and he demanded that his medical assistants be continuously changed.*

Several years passed, and Karma took this greedy person because he got sick with this particular disease. It wasn't until then that he understood that nothing but his famous surgery could help him. And here was the trouble—for he'd taught no one knew how to do such an operation!
This poor fellow died a couple of months later in suffering and remorse, realising what a terrible sin he had committed.

My example is very striking, but in everyday life, this law works every minute. If it seems that you have been offended or punished undeservedly, try to understand how you could provoke such a situation. In general, my advice to you is: Do not ask yourself the question, "Why?" Rather ask yourself, "What is this for?"

For what, vast universe, is there such a situation in my life? What should I understand or need to understand so that this does not happen again? What would prevent such people in my life from appearing? Ask these questions aloud and rest assured that the answer will come.

A sense of intuition and the ability to speak with the universe develops just as simply as other talents. For example, just like the ability to play the piano or draw, or dance, or cook. Practice and training allow us to achieve these tasks. You are the future Great Goddesses. Practice this task.

4. THE LAW OF INTERNAL PREPAREDNESS

This fourth law states that you must be internally prepared to achieve great success and significant accomplishments. Yes, in this circumstance I am talking about inner preparedness.

This means that you must be ready to accept the gifts of the universe so that they do not destroy you.

This law has many examples in history. Very often, people win millions in the lottery and then their life collapses because they were not ready for such a considerable amount of money. Many celebrities end their lives sick and alone or die from an overdose of alcohol and drugs because fame and success covered their heads like a massive wave in the ocean. Therefore, when you dream about fame, about money, and about external beauty, tell yourself, "Universe, help me to be internally ready to become great, to become beautiful, and to become smart and productive."

What does it mean to be prepared to accept all these gifts? **It means that all future changes will not change your soul or your behaviour.** You will remain a humble, loving soul, will treat others with huge respect, and you will be willing to help others when it is required. This lesson is crucial to remember.

Imagine you are sitting down watching TV. Suddenly, someone knocks on your door and says, "Here, have a bag of money. It is yours."

Instead of wandering around or squealing with happiness like a pig, you say, "Well, thank you. Please put the bag in that room. I will watch this exciting show on TV, and after that, I'll take care of this money."

You then finish watching the TV and go and take out **the exact amount of money that you need** from the bag. Next, you go shopping and **only** buy what you like and what you enjoy. Most importantly, you thank the universe for this opportunity. Then suddenly, the next morning the same person appears and says, "Sorry, we made a mistake. This bag of money was delivered to you by accident, and now I have to take it away."

You calmly answer, "Of course, please take it as you must." And you think to yourself, "Universe, thank you for a few days of unforgettable pleasures. **Nothing is everlasting in this world, and I am ready for all changes that may arise.**"

That is how future Great Goddesses will think.

5. THE LAW OF UNIVERSAL WISDOM

The fifth law refers to **being wise** from the young age. This is where we prepare sleds at the start of summer for the winter to come. It refers to where we need to save up for a rainy day. For example, if you observe squirrels gathering nuts, then you will soon notice that the first thing they will do is hide a few of them to eat in case they may not be able to find any other food that day. In other words, they are prepared for a rainy day.

You mustn't become an emotional spender. Save a quarter of your pocket money or part of a gift in case you need something urgently. In general, as future Great Goddesses, you will have to grow up early, and wise up at an early age. To be wise means to be a giver—a giver of good and a keeper of knowledge, family traditions, and home wealth. Good luck, future wise mothers of all mothers.

Listen to my story:

> *Before I begin, it is important to note that my story is from a time when parents were responsible for finding a spouse for their child. So, I will begin by saying that a father found his son a very modest, nice-looking woman from a poor family.*
> *The young couple started their life together. This young man worked as a truck driver and at the beginning of the last century, it was an incredibly good job to hold. He had money but never knew how much he made as every few days he put a mountain of crumpled dollars on the table, and his wife looked after them. One day he was pulled over by a policeman, and somehow, he was arrested for a crime that he did not commit. His wife came to visit him in jail, and*

he said, "There is no way I can be freed! The lawyer will require too much for his services. We will never be able to pay him!"

"How much will he cost?" asked his wife.

After the poor wretch told her how much it would cost, she smiled and said, "We have much more than that, my dear husband. I kept all your earnings and have never overspent. We have the money to save your life."

That was my grandma and grandpa. They had a long life together, full of prosperity and happiness. My grandma liked to give to others and to help her neighbours; however, in her secret box she always kept a stash of hidden money for "special occasions."

6. THE LAW OF CONSTANT MOVEMENT AND TRANSITION

The sixth law is the law of constant movement and the transition of energy from one species to another **in increasing order**, or more commonly referred to as **the law of the spiral.**

The existence of all life on this planet and in the entire universe is continuously changing and developing. Previous experience accumulates, and our being and consciousness are subsequently self-improving. This is called "Evolution". Both: the planets and the stars and all microscopic organisms undergo evolutional processes continuously.

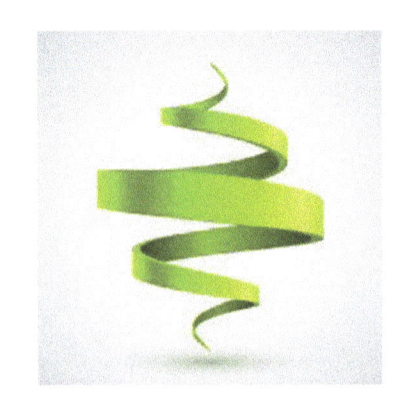

Did you know that viruses are the perfect creatures? They multiply every fifteen minutes. And each future generation is much smarter than the previous one. This is because they mutate at a tremendous speed, becoming "smarter and smarter." This is why, to this day, we still cannot create a cure for viral disease.

This law also controls our lives. We, as people, live specific cycles of life through which we are always developing. I'm not talking about physical growth here, but rather soul and spiritual growth, which also have their own life cycles.

In the first stage of development, there is **peaceful and accepting love** (I must point out that only women really know how to cultivate these feelings). As such, the first stage of development is the ability to feel and express boundless love for the world. One philosopher said, "Love is self-discipline in pleasure." In my mind, love is a feeling of harmony, happiness, and positivity. And I strongly believe that this feeling should become our daily habit.

Let's do an exercise called, "**A breath of joy.**" Imagine how you breathe when your most cherished dream comes true. Then, hold that moment in your mind and try to breathe like this for several minutes, several times a day. This will help you to develop the instinct of joy and harmony in your heart, because in this moment, you will be feeling love at a cellular level.

In the second stage of our development, we become **curious and have the capacity to adjust.** This illustrates a high level of interaction with the outside world and enables us to let go of the old without regret. All these qualities make us strong, independent personalities. It is also critical to master the ability to accept someone else's opinion peacefully and benevolently.

So be curious, my dear Goddesses, as curiosity is the leading quality of young people. Older people think "they know everything" and what they don't know they just don't want to know. A spiritual movement towards one's divine is possible but only through knowledge and with quick adaptation to the "new."

The third stage of development **is creativity.** After we have learned what love means and how to adapt to the world around us, we are ready to develop creativity in the name of love, in the name of improvement to this world, and in the lives of others. It is important to note that this creativity does not look for particular appreciation because we are unique, and creativity brings out our unique talent.

The fourth stage of development **is wealth.** It is the logical conclusion to the previous stages of love, curiosity, and creativity. It is also the last stage of human development and will naturally bring us success, prosperity, and material and spiritual wealth. These four stages are the first round toward establishing your spiritual growth. To improve on this, you will need to continue to develop—right through to the end of your life.

In general, life is an endless spiral. At each level, we start by loving ourselves and others as they are in peaceful acceptance of our environment. Following that, there is a natural desire for improvement, and as a result, glory and prosperity.

I hope my explanation is clear and to complement it, I would also like to give an example from Elon Musk. His life is a perfect explanation of true development from being a young, poor student loving his science, to a successful creator of many unbelievable projects.

CYCLE OF LIFE

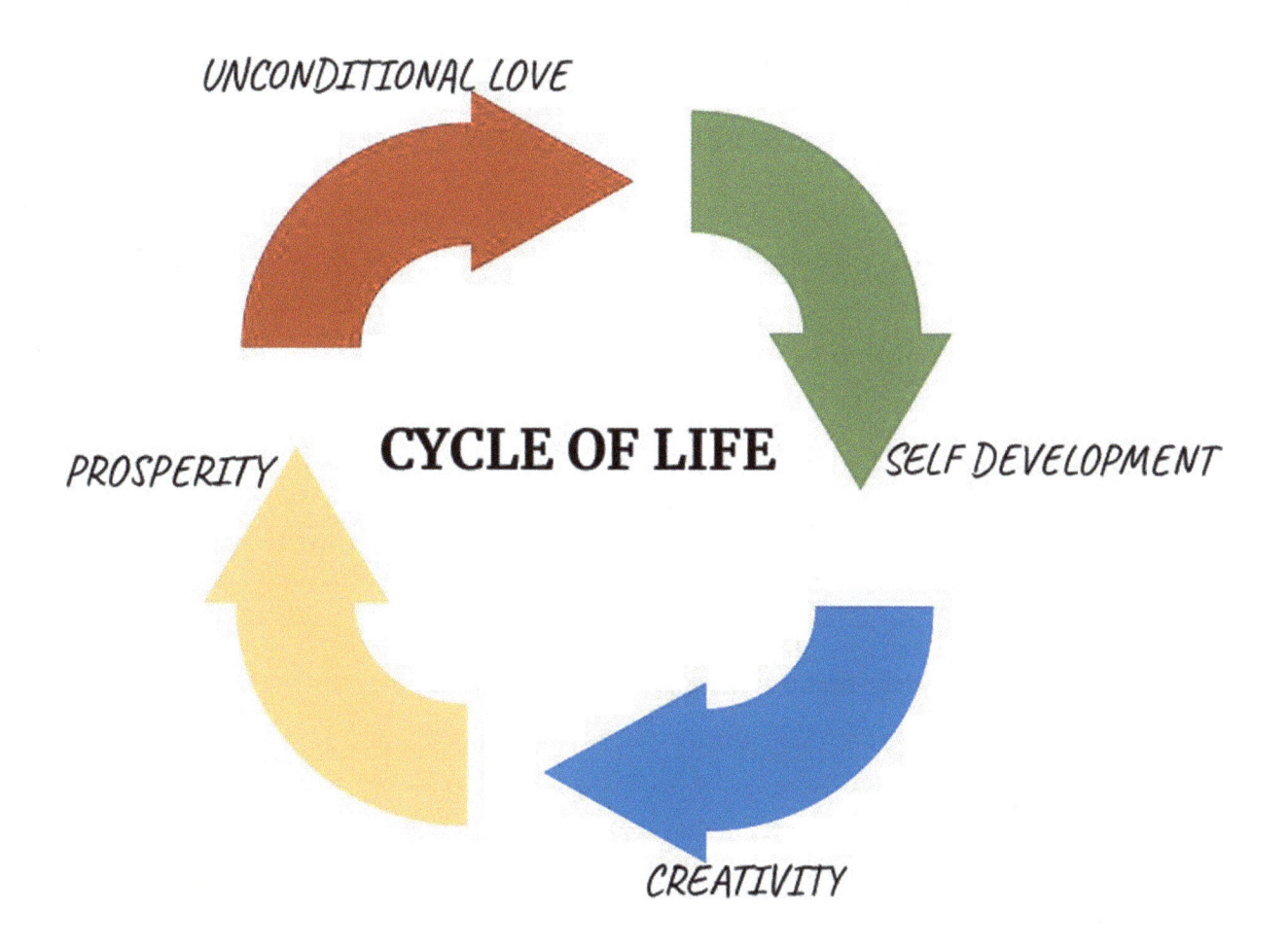

- UNCONDITIONAL LOVE
- SELF DEVELOPMENT
- CREATIVITY
- PROSPERITY

Please remember that you are unique, dear Goddesses. Remember that you have been created with a specific and essential goal, and our task is to understand and implement this goal. It is a sin not to use your talent. Listen to your heart and believe your intuition. When I was a little child and adults asked me what I wanted to become when I grew up, I answered, "When I grow up, I will help everyone." Being little, I did not know what profession this would be called, but it didn't matter because I had already felt my calling. And now, I am a nurse with twenty-two years of experience, and I still love helping people. This was, and still is, my mission!

Think about it, dear Goddesses. What is your calling?

As illustrated by the cycle of love in the diagram above, love for this world will be the beginning and the end of the path—and like a chain, once again, the beginning. Great Goddesses, love and be loved. **True love cannot spoil! But disrespect and arrogance can offend forever.**

7. THE LAW OF FREE CHOICE

In the universe, the number seven is considered a holy figure, bearing a lot of meaning and strength. Therefore, the seventh law of the universe is the law of free choice.

Every creature and every person have the right to freedom of choice. This is truly a great rule.

When you feel bad, my precious Goddesses, or when you are unhappy, look up to the sky and shout loudly and clearly, "I express my will that from this moment, my life is transformed. I will soon have worthy friends, a partner who will respect me, a beautiful body, a…" and so on. You understand how it works.

It is vital to put the power of your desire into words (as our boy did when he asked for his mother's health). It is essential to say what you want, Goddesses, and not what you DO NOT want. I encourage you as much as possible to not use the prefix, "don't."

And at the end of the expression of your will, you must say, "So be it, truly so. Amen."

That's all! You sent your order to the universe, and you secured it with a seal. Then, all you need to do is wait and be open to life's opportunities. So be it, indeed so!

Shakespeare said, "Life is a game." If one of my friends did not like a situation, she would say, "God, I do not want to play this game anymore!"

and the very next day, she was free of her problem. Of course, this happened because she verbalised her desire **willingly.**

So, practice, dear Goddesses, each and every day, and you will experience the freedom of choice. I wish you good luck!

A FEW ESSENTIAL TIPS:

Please respect older people.

Listen to my story:

I had a patient. His name was Daniel, and he was eighty-eight years old. I loved this grandfather, but he had dementia or what is commonly known as memory loss. He did not remember my name during the five years that I nursed him, and he often confused days and events, but in his youth, he was a surgeon. During the Second World War, he conducted his operations in the open field, sometimes only using a dull knife and sometimes without thread to sew up the operated organ. Over his entire fifty-year career as a military surgeon, not a single one of his patients died on his makeshift operating table. He saved thousands and thousands of lives.
Each time I visited this man, I felt sorry for him. He had changed from one of the most special doctors in the last century into a defenseless little man who had difficulties understanding simple things.

So, I want to give you some advice: Please respect older people. Even if they don't know what computers are or how to login to Facebook. Remember that they have a long and hard life behind them. Help them—not just your own family, but strangers too. Tell them how limitless your respect is towards them. Say it out loud and often. Many of them suffer unbearably in their old, sick bodies or from their helplessness or uselessness. Consult them for advice and they will surprise you with tips that you cannot read in an encyclopaedia or find on Google.

Please feel the pain of others

Here is another of my stories for my beautiful Goddesses:

> *When I first began nursing, I was a student in a hospital in Israel. My first patient was called, Rachel. This grandmother was extremely ill. Her legs had been amputated and her kidneys refused to work. She could not do anything by herself! I took care of her for a week, bathing her, feeding her, and helplessly watching her slowly fade away.*
> *One morning, I found her unconscious. She was not in a coma, but she was raving. I saw a grimace of pain distort her face, and I tried to make her more comfortable in her bed. She began to whisper something with all her strength. I tried very hard to listen carefully and to understand what it was that she was saying. Finally, I realised that she was whispering to me, "I am heavy. Do not lift me without help. Call for help." This poor grandmother, even while dying, was thinking of me—a young and healthy woman!*

My dear girls, this story should show you that it is important to take care of others and to feel someone's pain as your own. When you feel like you want to stab a lazy waitress, instead, just compliment her. Maybe she is hurting inside, or perhaps she is grieving about somebody at home. When shopping at the store, smile at the cashier. Say something beautiful from the bottom of your heart. Trust me, it will be appreciated. Whenever you are offended or disrespected, consider if this person might be having a terrible day. Maybe they don't always act this way so mentally wish them spiritual growth. **Remember that goodwill disarms.**

CONCLUSION

Remember that to be a Goddess does not mean to be omnipotently foolish. You have a massive responsibility for those who are spiritually younger than you are. Someone once told a wise man, "Oh my god, how smart you are!" The wise man smiled and answered modestly, "I'm not smart. I just understood something before you did. You will realise this yourself one day, too." This wise man was correct. There will always be someone more intelligent than we are. The road to excellence has no end.

Being young, we do not think about life eternal and that is fine. However, if you read this chapter, you will no doubt have some thoughts about your future. How would you like to see your life in five to ten years? What will you do for yourself to become better and happier person?

It was such a pleasure to chat with you, my dear girls. Be forever young, happy, and joyful in your soul. Have wisdom, intuition, and internal desire to transfer this planet into paradise. I wish you good luck.

With great respect and love,

Mama Nata.

NOTES AND REVELATIONS

2

WHAT IS GOD'S DESIGN?

This chapter will be dedicated to the beautiful female body and the simple laws of health, youth, and beauty. I have also included techniques for cleansing our bodies.

Why did I decide that this topic is relevant today? Because we live in an era of genetically modified foods, complete illiteracy of the existing health care system, the Gestapo pharmacology, and the tyranny of vaccinations. **Our health is our responsibility.** In the previous century, we had famous doctors like Sergey Botkin, who discovered Hepatitis A, B, and C, and we also had Doctor Karl Landsteiner, who discovered the blood groups and RH. These doctors were a blessing and helped to save lives. Unfortunately, we have less and less of these real, thinking medical providers today.

I am sorry that due to people's silent agreement, you, our children, are forced to grow up in the murky world of careless businesses that manipulate our lives and our health. I feel humiliated.

I spoke to our creator, and I asked him once, " My lovely Lord! Why did you give us such beautiful bodies but failed to provide us with instructions on how to use them?" The creator answered, "Here you go, why don't you write the instructions?" And suddenly, it all made sense.

Why do we endlessly ask him for help? Maybe, instead, we need to imagine a different picture, Old Grandpa, sitting in the sky? He has listened for so many years to all of us that he doesn't know who to listen to first. Now, instead of begging, I raise my head, look up to the sky and say, "My beloved Grandpa, how can I help you? What can I do for you?"

Essentially, this is why I am trying to write the " instructions" for using our body and to warn you against possible health problems. I am also trying to teach you the basics to properly care for your body. It is impossible to fit all that you will need to know in this book (we will have more books, we will become professors of The Health Academy gradually), but let's assume that this chapter is your first set of instructions for a vast, multi-functional biological machine. My readers may be nine years old (and I will not be surprised givenhow quickly girls can mature!), or maybe nineteen. However, it does not matter what age you are, as this information is applicable as soon as you are old enough to comprehend it. So, I speak to you all, my future Goddesses, with great respect and in simple terms—just like my grandmother did when I was a child. May the Lord help you to understand me, and I hope that you feel all the love and genuine care that I hold for you, my beautiful sunshine.

To begin, let's imagine that our body is like a tree.

Just as there are roots, a trunk, branches, leaves, flowers, and fruits on a tree, so too are there such things in our body. It is a brilliant, branched system consisting of billions of microscopic cells. Our roots are our body cells; their duty is to supply our body (or the whole tree) with energy, nutrition, and moisture. Our trunk includes our circulatory systems, our lymphatic system, and our intestines. The juices of life run along them and nourish our branches, which are our organs. And if our branches (which include the liver, kidneys, lungs, the pancreas and other organs) receive proper nutrition, then the foliage of our tree looks healthy and flowering. Now, imagine that the leaves are our skin, our nails, and our hair. If our body is healthy and if everything is in its natural order, then these, too, will shimmer and radiate light and joy.

Now imagine a tree in our garden which has begun to fade and turn yellow. This is where you would call a gardener. The gardener would come, assess the tree, and say, "Let's grease the yellow leaves with cream and tie them with a ribbon to the branch so that they do not fall." Would you believe such a gardener? I don't think so. We will likely invite another gardener to assess the tree. The second gardener says, "The tree needs more water (or less, it depends on the type of tree), more (or less) sun and fertilisers, and **the tree will recover itself.** In some cases, some branches may need to be chopped off, and new branches will subsequently grow."

So, why do we believe those doctors who treat only the lungs, or only the kidneys, or only the pinkie on the left foot instead of looking at the whole body? I want you to understand, dear Goddesses, that our bodies are not isolated islands like in the Boundless Ocean. Everything is connected to everything. **Disease and old age do not exist if there is no violation of the internal harmony of the body.**

VIOLATIONS OF THE LAWS OF NATURE

Diseases arise as a result of violations of the laws of nature—those of which we have already talked a lot about above. These disorders first appear at the energy level, and if we continue to waste our life energy and do not restore it, illness arises. Thus, fixing these energy levels will help our body work flawlessly and for an exceedingly long time.

That said, the universal causes of all diseases are without exception:

- Lack of love and feelings of loneliness
- Fear and resentment
- Constant stress and a sense of competition, including the futile pursuit of first place and maintaining social standards
- Lack of sleep
- Contaminated blood and lymphatic systems
- Chronic constipation, greed, drug, and alcohol use, and
- Chronic dehydration and starvation of the cells

It is worth noting that the first three **are mental or emotional** but they play a very important role in our **physical** problems.

Our body is an invaluable gift from the universe that is worthy of respect and admiration. It is a sacred temple of soul development, and the first step to health protection is **paying careful attention to our bodies.** If you have already noticed, my beautiful Goddesses, why your stomach hurts after a particular food, then do not eat that food! If you come to realise that certain people are causing you to develop a headache, do not communicate with them. If you see a man on the roof of his house trying to disperse the clouds in the sky with a whisk instead of fixing a roof, what would you think? That he's crazy? Exactly!

Be observant, my dear Goddesses. After all, each of you is unique, beautiful, and perfect. So, work on yourself.

We will work on our life habits, our diet, and our attitude first. Trust me when I say that your body will thank you and respond with endless possibility.

To repair the roof, you must improve yourself without complaining about the clouds (or the world around us). I would like to share several of Nikola Tesla's tips with you. This incredible man was a famous scientist who invented the alternating electric system, magnetic fields, and much more. He was an incredibly talented man and his advices will be relevant for many generations. Tesla's following tips will help you to work on yourself.

1. **The important thing is not the love that we receive from others, but the love that we give.** Hurry up to love, ladies, to obtain a sense of peace and goodness in our hearts.

2. **The gift of mental clarity comes from God, and you will find it within wise books.** Enjoy classic books written by Maupassant, Romain Rolland, Leo Tolstoy, and more. Reading is important because the more we know, the more secure we become. And only through unexpected insights do we become aware of our limitations and find great truth. Do not be afraid to be alone, my dolls, with the loneliness, inspiration will visit you more often.

3. **Before any act, a desire to fulfil it must first appear. The more passionate this desire becomes, the sooner and easier that goal will be achieved.** Wish passionately, Goddesses. Be emotional and unlimited with your ambitions. DREAMS MUST BE UNRESTRICTED! SO, DREAM BIG!

4. **Our shortcomings and advantages are inseparable. If they are divided, a person cannot exist. Girls, love your flaws as well as your virtues.** Do not judge yourself severely, and of course, do not judge others either.

This was the advice of the great scientist, Nikola Tesla. Follow these tips, my Goddesses, and I hope they will help you overcome your fears and resentments and help you resist the desperation of loneliness.

CONTAMINATED BLOOD AND THE LYMPHATIC SYSTEMS

Now, we will move on to the physical causes of health problems. Our blood, lymphatic system, and all the fluids in our body are a natural environment for the growth of numerous fungi, viruses, parasites, and worms.

So, what does "contaminated blood systems" and "lymphatic systems" actually mean? You must understand that we all have millions of living organisms in our bodies. All of these living organisms drain our health and life energy, whereas some even try to control us or our thoughts. Therefore, simple and regular cleansing of the blood and lymphatic system is crucial. And thankfully, nature takes care of us. Mother nature has created many cleansing herbs that can keep our body fluids clean. Nowadays, there are many professional naturopaths and homeopaths, and if you are lucky, you may have come across an educated doctor who cares about your health. Always have a specialist whom you trust, and one in which you can conduct competent, intelligent dialogue. Meanwhile, knowledge is available on the Internet, so do not be lazy and read!

Nature provides us with a bounty and the following is an easy, natural recipe that you can use to clean your blood and lymphatic system. But naturally, please consult with your parents and a trusted healthcare provider first.

MY FAVOURITE CLEANSING TEA

This tea will detox your blood and your lymphatic system from viruses, bacteria, fungi, and other living organisms that continuously hurt us. This tea is tasty, healthy, and indispensable during epidemics of viruses and colds.

Ingredients:

5 ltr of water

300-400 gr of ginger root,

5-6 whole lemons with peels

20-30 clove seeds

5-6 bay leaves

Method:

1. Wash everything thoroughly.

2. Bring everything to a boil and simmer for two-three minutes.

3. Turn off the heat.

4. Add three to five tablespoons of each: dried chamomile, nettle, red clover, and sage to this broth.

5. Steep for one to two hours, then like tea, drink it several times a day before meals, in a glass. You may keep this tea in the refrigerator for few weeks, it will be even better with time.

OVEREATING AND CONSTIPATION

This is a serious topic. This illness is deadly and highly prevalent today. Elvis Presley and Marilyn Monroe died of constipation. From constipation comes dozens of other diseases that doctors cannot cure. Many issues are being treated with antibiotics, steroids, and surgeries, and doctors are very rarely interested in a person's eating habits.

Now, I will explain to you, my beautiful girls, what constipation is. It is not always associated with the amount of the stool, but rather with its consistency. You must go to the bathroom at least two to three times a day. The stool should be very soft, almost liquid at the end. It is also necessary to pay attention to the appearance of your tummy; it should be flat and soft and painless if you squeeze it a little.

Constipation is entirely dependent on our diet and the habit of drinking water. Of course, there are more serious problems, too, but I am not giving medical advice here. Aggressive and frequent constipation requires professional intervention, such as through a gastroenterologist who is a specialist of the stomach and intestines.

Now, I will explain to you what diarrhoea is. Diarrhoea is when a stool looks almost like water. Diarrhoea can be of different colours, with a fetid odour, or with mucus. I do not think it is worth stopping diarrhoea as this is an emergency cleansing of the body. However, it is advisable to stop eating and only drink mineral water, or water with lemon and honey. If there is severe pain in the abdomen or severe weakness, then get your family to take you to an emergency room. But if diarrhoea is without pain and it doesn't bother you, then drink and cleanse yourself.

Start your morning with a few tablespoons of good quality olive oil or coconut oil. Drink warm water in the morning and eat little or nothing. If you do decide to eat, choose plums or drink kefir. Let the stomach wake up first.

The uncultured, heavy breakfast is floury. It usually consists of toast, then sweets, then orange juice, and the devil knows what else there is in those sugar-filled cereal boxes that shock the intestines. The very first meal should be eaten at noon when the sun is in the zenith, and also when our hormones are at their peak and the body needs energy.

My dear girls, try to cultivate healthy eating habits from a young age. Eat a fresh meal at least once a day. By fresh, I mean vegetables and fruits, instead of sandwiches and sweets. In fact, raw food including fresh vegetable salads must comprise 80% of your diet. Please learn to love plain vegetables with good olive oil to get the most benefit from them. The best vegetables are spinach, carrots, cucumber, onion, parsley, tomato, and avocado. Please, do not overuse mayonnaise, sugars, or other chemicals. Lemon juice (real, squeezed lemon) will add so much to your salad!

Chew as carefully and slowly as you can, eating while in a good mood. Do not seize anger and resentment as this will make your butt grow like it's being fertilised!

It is best to drink thawed water. Enchant your water , wish yourself health and success, then drink it.

There is nothing wrong with the ability to work with energies. You are Goddesses! One esoteric said, "Magic is the art of controlling power by focusing attention to bring changes in reality." That's all, nothing devilish in here.

There are ways to detox your body from overeating. This includes **the mono-diet.** A mono-diet is where you eat no more than one or two foods across the course of the day. This helps you to lose weight quickly. You should mono-diet for only one to two days and choose foods like bananas and avocado. You can also unload your digestive system by eating a very simple diet of water and fresh homemade juice for a day or two.

Nutrition at the cellular level is different from food at the stomach level. Not everything we eat will benefit our bodies. With this being said, modern reality is the tragedy of greed and ubiquitous noise. From the 400 grams of food we consume, our stomach can hardly digest forty. The rest will lie as dead weight in the intestines. And cells need only twenty-one amino acids for healthy activity, (three of them are fatty amino acids--Omega 3 for example), twenty-three vitamins, seventy-four minerals, and eleven enzymes. My point is, we eat in different levels—in the stomach level and in the cell level. Sometimes our stomach is full, and we literally cannot breathe, but after forty to forty-five minutes our cells crave WHAT THEY NEED. A necessary signal will be sent to the brain, and the brain will tell us to go and eat more because the cells are still hungry.

This is a dangerous circle because we eat more of the same useless food (like hamburgers and huge sandwiches), and as such, our cells become more and more hungry. We subsequently eat more only to find that our cells are still in need of the same twenty-one amino acids, twenty-three vitamins, seventy-four minerals, and eleven enzymes.

The catch here is that you need to know how and where to get the food your cells need. And the purpose of our conversation is to emphasize the importance of mindful nutrition. Once again, my precious, feel your body. Eat nutritiously. Do not make a trash can out of your stomach (this means no chips, no sugar cane food, be careful with milk products, and make sure you don't have a lactose allergy). Again, **feel your body.**

I hope that I haven't scared you too much as this really is simple. Just as every car needs a specific type of gasoline, our cells need specific ingredients for growth and development. Find such a specialist, but also educate yourself.

For a better appreciation of our multi-system body, here are a few facts to remember:

1. The brain burns 30% of the body's calories and 25% of the body's oxygen. It is continuously growing new neurological connections. Most brain disorders arise from some deficiency or toxicity. Both risk factors may be prevented by correct diet and daily, natural remedies that detox and renew the lymphatic system, blood, and GI systems.

2. Brain cell vibration entirely depends on our diet. This comes from four waves: Alfa, Beta, Tetra, and Delta. We hardly use any of these waves but only the Beta waves alone. To be able to reach the highest level of IQ and EQ, we need to use all four streams.

3. Wherever our attention is being directed, so will our energy and brain vibration be addressed. Then all of life will be headed there.

4. A raw diet should comprise 80% of total meals and may be the best solution for the majority of our health problems. Eating fresh food daily will activate natural processes in our body including cell renewal and detoxification. A raw diet increases energy levels, improves the immune system, and normalises the PH level in our bloodstream.

5. The most common disease nowadays is the "leaky gut." Leaky gut is caused by eating GENETICALLY MODIFIED FOOD. This condition brings many physical and mental disorders like chronic pain, systemic inflammations, autism, and even dementia at a young age. **We must learn how to read labels.**

6. Our liver filters more than two litres of blood each minute, and controls about twenty different vital body functions. The Ancient Greeks considered the liver to be the centre of our body. To have good health means having a healthy liver i.e. no alcohol and fast food is allowed.

7. Many vitamin and mineral deficiencies will mimic the most severe physical and mental diseases and may be treated with a beneficial diet.

8. Water has ten essential qualities. Drinking water that has all of these categories will give our body cells a considerable push of energy and extraordinary abilities on both physical and mental levels.

In summary, 80% of your diet should comprise of raw foods. I also encourage you to sleep with the window open, keep your room without carpets, and if possible, without soft toys. Try not to watch TV, and by this, I mean meaningless movies and/or stupid shows. In summer, swim in the sea and walk barefoot on the ground. Fast one day a week to cleanse your intestines, and warm up your liver and lower abdomen with an electric heating pad while sleeping at night. Ensure the temperature is pleasantly warm as this is very beneficial for the female body. I also encourage you to try to prevent stressful situations (if possible). Remember, my precious girls, a woman who takes care of herself will always find a person who will appreciate and respect her.

In this chapter, we went over a range of issues relating to your body. These are all very important, my dear girls, so I hoped you paid attention.

You are lucky girls; you will live in the fifth dimension. Great Elena Blavatsky predicted all that is happening now in the 1880s in her book, The Secret Doctrine. The electromagnetic fields around our planet have changed, which means that the universe is now actively working on creating a new human. You were born in a great time and you are highly spiritual humans. Your thoughts and behaviour will have meaningful contact with the universe and nature—just like the tree that we talked about above. I will not be surprised if, in twenty years, people will begin to understand the language of animals, birds, and flowers. And I've no doubt that **it will be you !**

You, the Goddesses of the future, will remember your rights and freedom of personal choice, you will strive for personal growth, and sovereignty. You will live in love and harmony with the Mother Earth and its inhabitants. You will begin to create a new reality, completely different from the primitive duality in which humanity has existed up till this point. Each and every one of you is the future centre of divine universal energy, the centre of all forgiveness and all understanding. You will put an end to hard work and mental slavery. You will live your life fully revealing your vast inner potential and deep divine purpose. Your reality will be full of endless miracles and fabulous successes, eternal health, and youth.

YES, IT WILL BE SO!

I express my will so that it will happen.

With great respect,

Truly yours,

Mama Nata

NOTES AND REVELATIONS

3

THE GREATNESS IN SMALL AND DETAILS OF THE GREAT

My dear Goddesses, in the third chapter we will talk about the energies of a woman, specifically in terms of how to feel them, and how to work with them.

The woman is a divine vessel of universal energy. In ancient times, men believed that their real communication with God, and with the cosmos, could only happen through a woman. Subsequently, throughout history, women have been continuously underestimated and even shamed and intimidated by aggressive and oppressive behaviours of powerful men. The Inquisition, by itself, has destroyed millions of strong, freethinking women. But the purpose of this chapter is only to provide a small introduction, so, we'll talk about female energy and how to create it, how to clean it, how to work with it, and how to use it.

ENERGY CENTRES OF THE HUMAN BODY

You may have already heard that there are many energy centres associated with the human body. These centres have particular importance and are responsible for the healthy flow of our energies throughout the body. There are seven majors centres, but there are also many smaller ones.

The first energetic centre is responsible for survival and for blocking the feeling of fear. This centre is located where our body makes contact with the earth as we sit. If the centre works correctly, then a person feels love for life and for his body. When it is blocked, a person constantly feels tired, hostile, and has low self-esteem. **This centre is associated with the element of earth.**

The second energetic centre is responsible for joy and blocks feelings of guilt. A person enjoys life and enjoys physical pleasure as, for example, eating. When communication in this centre is not blocked. But when the centre is blocked, a person becomes full of suspicion and distrust. **This centre is located below the abdomen and is associated with the element of water.**

The third energetic centre is responsible for willpower and blocks unnecessary feelings of shame. A person is usually peaceful and full of ambitious goals and will quickly attain status and wealth, but when this centre is blocked, a person behaves like a despot. He is not self-confident and he condemns everyone and everything. **This centre is located at the navel level and is associated with the element of fire.**

The fourth energetic centre is responsible for selfless love and therefore, blocks sorrow. A person is full of joy, he is peaceful and friendly to all living things. When this centre is open, we bloom as a beautiful rose of mercy and forgiveness. But when this centre is blocked, we are always offended and disappointed. **This energy centre is located next to our heart and is associated with the element of the sun.**

The fifth energetic centre is responsible for the truth and helps to block lies. If you have friends who express their gratitude quickly and openly and know how to speak calmly in public places, this means that their fifth energy centre is open. If there are blocks in this centre, people will argue for no reason, will often get upset, and will say that they have "a lump stuck in their throat". That is not surprising given this energy centre is at the level of our throat. **This centre is associated with the element of sound.**

The sixth energetic centre is responsible for insight, intuition, courteous behaviour, and the ability to see through the veiled acts and hidden flaws of others. This centre blocks illusions and disunity. This means that if this centre is undeveloped, the person will be unsociable, negative, hostile to others, and will also consider himself as a dumbass. **This centre is at the bridge of the nose, between the eyes, where Indian women paint their moles and is associated with the element of light.**

The seventh energetic centre is the last big one and is the centre of the cosmic energy responsible for the connection with the universe. Here, we receive powerful cosmic energy which helps us to not focus on material pleasures too much. The open centre gives us divine love and a sense of inner harmony. If this centre is blocked, people have an overestimated ego and become selfish, and as a result, very lonely. **This centre is located on the crown of the human head and is associated with the element of the universe.**

Through all these centres, energy moves from Mother Earth to the universe and back. This means we are all walking conductors of energy, like biological batteries.

To have these centres opened, we should spend time enjoying water (rivers, lakes, ocean), fire (bonfires sun), light (sunrise and sunset), colours (rainbow, flowers, beautiful birds), and sound (music, laughter). Mother Nature has all we need, so enjoy every gift that God created for us. Some people feel that yoga is extremely helpful; some like meditation. Discover this for yourself.

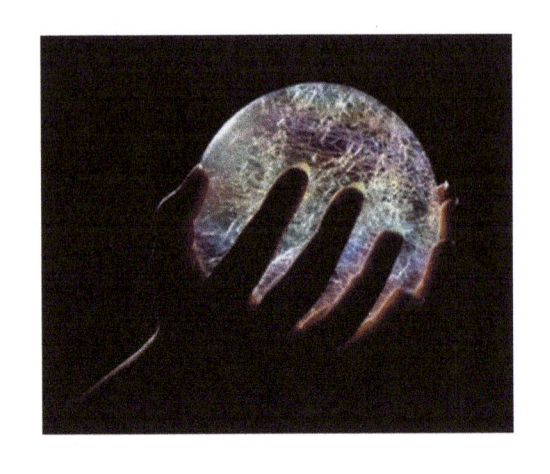

TYPES OF ENERGIES

So, what type of energies pass through our bodies?

There are so many types, including electric, magnetic, torsion, fountain, magical, soul, spiritual, mental, emotional, and intelligent. Because of this, we are complex creatures. The power of these energy waves depends on age, state of health, emotional intensity, and many other factors. And of course, a woman is a battery with deadly force, just by the fact of her creation.

Also, energies can be high-frequency and low-frequency. Examples of high-frequency energy are joy, mercy, compassion, tenderness, goodwill, insight, and love. And low-frequency energies are energies of destruction, including fear, resentment, loneliness, aggression, and distrust. These energies must be recognised and cancelled, otherwise, after a while, autoimmune diseases begin to develop in the body (such as hypothyroidism, arthritis, and diabetes) which have almost no treatment options. In effect, the body destroys itself.

And now the main question is, how can we raise our energies and become highly energetic people?

First of all, by breathing. Let's start breathing with a pause. Inhale a deep, slow breath through the nose, pause for thirty seconds, and then slowly exhale through the mouth. This exercise should be done several times a day. As soon as a lump of anger or fear enters the throat, say out loud, "I forgive and let go of this situation. So, let it be." It is not easy, but after several tries, I guarantee that it will work.

The next technique is sound and rhythm. Try to use singing bowls, bells, shaman's tambourines, or conversely, listen to soothing music, Indian mantras, or to the birds singing. And if you also sing and dance, it is the perfect solution to all low energy level problems.

Another strategy is working with water. Thawed ice is clean water in terms of energy and information. Begin by stirring a glass of melted ice water with a spoon clockwise, as if we are stirring sugar in it. It will turn into a funnel. Speak into this funnel all that we want to happen. Remember to reiterate our expression of will to the universe. For example, "I am the love. I am the mercy. I am the beauty. I choose peace, and I choose love. I accept the good, so let it be true. Amen!" Then, following this expression of will, drink the water. Do this experiment for forty days and miracles will start to happen.

Another strategy is thermotherapy. The female body loves light heat very much. Light warming of the lower abdomen and lower back, or soft warming of the perineum will open lower energetic centres. Girls, sleep with an electric heating pad to warm up your energy centres, all seven of them.

TORSION ENERGY

Torsion energy refers to the energy of a vortex. If you have ever seen a tornado, then you will understand what I'm talking about. We create vortex energys when we spin clockwise or rotate our wrist in a clockwise direction at the level of each energy centre for a couple of minutes. The power of this movement cannot be overestimated. Together, with internal work on ourselves and by listening to music and singing, we can work well on our energies with the help of torsion vortices. From my personal experience, the centre of female energy is at the level of our womb. In general, our uterus is a divine organ, full of universal power with an incredible connection to the whole world. But we'll talk about this a bit later.

The reason why I mentioned our uterus is that I would like to explain another method for improving our energy levels. Ask your mother to buy you a woman's scarf, the type that our grandmothers used to wear on their shoulders, as we need one for this strategy work. As often as possible, go for a walk in the countryside either in a forest, around the lake, at the seashore, or even in your backyard. If the weather allows, take off your shoes (by being barefoot, you will discover that it doesn't matter how cold it is outside, Mother Earth is always warm!), then take this scarf and ask the sun, the forest, the sea, and the fields with flowers to share with you their universal energy. After that, scoop it up with the scarf, and pull this power towards your belly. Do this seven times. After that, tie the scarf around your hips and walk around with it for several hours. Nature will have been happy to share its energy with you.

By the way, do you know why the skin on our feet and hands differ from the rest of our body? These places are our points of connection to energy sources. Dear princesses, walk barefoot and raise your soles to the sky. At this moment, you are just like a river along which the energy of the earth flows into space and back. You are a walking Amazon river!

I hope my advice was not very dull. I have really enjoyed introducing the subject of our energy and energetic possibilities. If you would like to find out more, please refer to my second book in this series, The art of becoming a Goddess.

Thank you, my darlings!

Sincerely yours,

Mama Nata.

NOTES AND REVELATIONS

4

IF YOUTH KNEW AND OLD AGE COULD

Many times I have heard from my friends, or often said too, "What a pity! If only I knew this before!" Therefore, I want to talk to you, my great Goddesses, about the power of knowledge. Pay attention to the fact that my goal here is to get you to understand that knowledge is different from education and that this is a powerful weapon.

You are so young and beautiful, my dear girls. This is great! But at the same time, you are so naive and trusting—so vulnerable. I close my eyes and imagine a small child crossing the highway without a traffic light or pedestrian crosswalk. I see this kid trying to slip between flying cars, and my heart skips a beat from fear. These are the feelings I experience when I think of you, my children, living in a modern, unfriendly society full of mentally inadequate people who are often not people at all.

The purpose of my life today is to warn you, my dear Girls, against the situations that can leave a bitter taste in your mouth—and even irreversible consequences in your lives and your souls. Some dangerous life situations can be foreseen and prevented simply by having specific knowledge. My grandmother called this the "School of Life." This is knowledge that a mother transfers to her daughter, who then transfers it to her daughter, and so on. This is knowledge that is not taught at school.

Please, dear Goddesses, I hope you understand why I am alarmed and believe me when I say that valid advice can save us from serious life mistakes. Of course, I'm aware that it is impossible to protect you from all of life's problems (and this should not be done given life should consist of issues and difficulties that make us stronger and wiser). But here, we are talking about irreparable errors and the role of broad knowledge as a real opportunity to protect ourselves from avoidable mistakes. I wish for you to have the ability to accumulate in-depth, multilateral knowledge and to be able to use it correctly and promptly in situations where the need arises.

I will share how you can accumulate this knowledge. Everyone knows that the internet and books are good sources of information. And it is here that we begin to get confused about several terms including information, education, and knowledge. Let's clarify the critical difference between all of them first.

Let's say we want to make a salad. We have tomatoes, cucumbers, radishes, eggs, onions, avocados, and herbs. These products are pure information. A ready-made salad is education (or a field of narrow specialisation such as doctors, actors, and economists). But the ability to cook several dishes from these products, and also come up with your own dish, is **the knowledge**.

Knowledge, I would say, is a rough diamond that everyone polishes in their own way after learning how to work with it. I look at this as our life experience. But the background to this is a period spent living in the world, and knowledge is the result of personal development which consists of everyday work on yourself.

Therefore, the first important rule here is to ensure that you **gather knowledge from several different sources.** In the example with the salad, go to the garden and pick tomatoes and cucumbers by yourself. Gather understanding as you would gather mushrooms in the woods or seashells on the beach. It is crucial to hear different points of view on an issue. And after you have listened to several answers to your question, use your critical thinking to decide INDEPENDENTLY on what valid advice is and what is not.

In addition to the sources of information that we have today i.e. the internet, books, and various courses and schools, I would like to introduce you to other sources of knowledge which are more truthful and still exciting. Yes, I am talking about the older generation. It's a great pleasure to listen to their stories. I have been doing this every day for the past seven years, not to mention the fact that my precious grandmother raised me, and I thoroughly enjoyed listening to her every day. She is my best friend and protector, and now she is my guardian angel. I know it for sure.

Another unique source of knowledge is found through "lucid dreaming.". In a simple sense, lucid dreams are accomplished by strategies. You learn how to ask your question and then go to sleep. While sleeping, you will receive an answer through your dream. Nowadays, there are tons of courses online which can teach you this specific skill. I highly recommend it. We will talk about that more in my next books.

While dreaming, we can reach the deepest level of memory in our bodies' cells. The monks from Tibet describe it as the book of Akasha. The great Edgar Cayce, Nikola Tesla, Mikhail Lomonosov, and many other scientists worked by using lucid dreaming. As do I, for while lucid dreaming, I receive unique ideas about how to treat my patients.

Success is guaranteed to those who can turn the ability of self-education or self-development into EVERYDAY HABIT, and those who IMMEDIATELY TEST THE RECOMMENDED PRACTICES. Although, I have to admit that such people are few. Ninety percent of the population will fall asleep in the first ten minutes of the most interesting lecture in the world and/or will forget about the tips they heard in a couple of hours. But this is not you—you are the Goddesses!

Things that interest you right now will make you successful, prosperous, and happy in the future. Please note, I do not ask you to relate to specific knowledge here, but rather in terms of KNOWING. Life is not a constant competition with a continuous struggle for first place. Our goal is to obtain the knowledge that will serve us in everyday life. Knowledge will help us to become protected and self-confident, and it will represent real VALUE to those around us.

If you remember my example of mushrooms and seashells in the topic we spoke of earlier, you would note that we do not collect everything that is lying under our feet. Girls, SELECTION is the ability to see what the main thing is, and conversely, what is secondary in life. This also allows us to see things in the right proportions. Do not waste your beautiful life on unnecessary diplomas and extra informational garbage just for the sake of wanting to please others, or because it is trendy (note that I did not mention the zombie box a.k.a TV). Do not fill your beautiful heads with different sorts of nonsense; **take care of the ecology of your inner world from an early age.** Your inner world should not be like the garage of an old bachelor.

You are vitally important as an individual. First of all, you are the witch that casts a spell with your intellect, your inner culture, and the unique and peculiar aroma of your inner self—which in the future will fascinate your friends and disinfect your enemies (remember that enemies usually outnumber friends).

SUMMARY:

In summary, we have talked about the fact that knowledge is an infinitely valuable tool that allows us to be:

1. Protected from everyday liars and irrational decisions

2. Happy and confident

3. Successful because we learn to be curious and to find the information we need quickly and correctly

4. Able to select information and categorise it into what is important to me and what is not important to me

We also talked a little bit about how and where we can get knowledge. This included from:

1. Books, educational magazines, and lectures online

2. Stories and advice from older people, especially relatives, whom we trust

3. From our dreams and intuition, with the ability to observe everything that surrounds us OBJECTIVELY without any emotion.

Therefore, it is time to decide what knowledge is the most important. Let's say, necessary. Here is an example:

Let's divide our understanding into the following:

1. Health and body care.

2. The correct behaviour i.e. healthy habits including the ability to listen and hear others, to speak politely, to show respect to others, and to create your own unique, internal flavour. This also includes standing up for yourself and protecting yourself from irreparable mistakes.

3. Relations and expression of feelings. Our female soul is not a public toilet where everyone is allowed to come and shit. Right?!

4. Life success, a woman's career (a very multifaceted term!), and professional pleasure.

5. Material wealth and primary financial education.

6. Spiritual development, physical development, and activation of cell memory.

7. Pure human curiosity or those aspects that interest you as a person and a future mother. (In my understanding, a mother is not the one who gave birth and raised children, but the one that grows to the level of receiving real pleasure from selfless service to the world around her.)

I hope you agree with me, my smart girls. If there are those of you who disagree, well done! Build your independent categories in which you will slowly but continuously collect and cultivate your own unique knowledge. I wish for all of you to become discerning fashionistas who will jealousy fill your basket of expertises with the perfect jewellery that you desire. Let it be so. Truly so!

Now, let's talk about each category of valuable knowledge.

1. HEALTH AND OUR BODY.

At a young age, we are all so beautiful! We are full of energy, we can eat everything, and we don't need to sleep much at night to feel good. Enjoy it.

But remember, without some work and the creation of several healthy habits, old age and illness will come into our lives without invitation. By the way, old age in medical language is chronic dehydration plus chronic acidification of the body. Yes, we are now talking about the physical body rather than the spiritual one.

Remember, dear Goddesses, to drink a glass of water half an hour before each meal. Ensure that this water is charged with positive energies, clean, and at a pleasant temperature. Drink the water slowly, obtain pleasure from it, and generally **get used to do everything with joy**. It is also worth drinking some water before bedtime and after physical contact with your loved one.

Eat green fruits and vegetables as much as possible. Green is the colour of our planet, the colour of mother nature. Green vegetables also fight acidification of the body. Yellow vegetables carry vitamin A; red is rich in vitamin E; cabbage of any kind will give us vitamin C; and all together, vitamins A, E, C are antioxidants (a long, dull word). In other words, they are anti-aging and immunity supportive vitamins. A fresh salad with virgin olive oil will give you a healthy intestine and plenty of Omega 3 which is necessary for the brain, hormonal system, and skin, and it will also put you in a good mood.

At least once a week, check your skin for irritations, excessive dryness, or itching. Check your stomach once a day with light pressure. Ensure there is no pain and that the tummy rumbles when you are hungry. Be careful not to overeat. Pay attention to puffiness under the eyes (which can be a symptom of a lack of sleep, overload, or even kidney disease). Check the odour of your urine as it is not supposed to elicit a sharp smell or precipitate. Pay attention to the condition of your stools. Watch out for constipation, pain, and mucus or blood in the stool.

Our body consists of many systems of self-regulation and self-healing; it talks to us and sends us signs if something is wrong. Pain, temperature, weakness, trembling, poor skin condition, despondency, and irritation are all the language of our body and not just independent diseases. It is worth listening to these symptoms rather than popping painkillers and anti-inflammatory, fever-reducing drugs. Remind your doctors if they forget this.

Remember, my dear Goddesses, that you are the future mothers even if you don't think about this right now. If not, miracles can happen, and if you decide to embrace motherhood, it is important to take care of your female organs by not sitting on cold stones. Rather, wear warm underwear in cold weather as you may obtain Pelvic Inflammatory Disease (or PID). This is a serious disease as the treatment of PID is an exceptionally long and painful process, and full recovery is sometimes impossible.

So, dear Goddesses, I encourage you to read the cognitive literature to develop your knowledge about natural types of treatment for mild colds, common health problems, nutrition, and detoxificating systems. All this advice will save you from cellulite on the bum at the age of seventeen, obesity, unnecessary pain, and wasting time and money to see a doctor. It is worth remembering that in the last century, every self-respecting family used to subscribe to magazines about health. These magazines were read and re-read and gathered over the years.

Let me share a few magic facts about our bodies. The human inner world is comprised of the genitourinary system which includes the uterus, ovaries, kidneys, and bladder. It is the repository of the entire memory of the earth and cosmos, holding unlimited potential. For example, the kidneys are the energy of time. The right kidney is the energy of the future; the left is the energy of the past. And the ovaries carry information of your family kind. The right ovary is passive information, accumulated from your previous generations. The left ovary is the information that you will collect through your life. Sounds as a mistery, right? Explore your body , we will talk about that in my next book more.

THE FEMALE UTERUS.

The uterus is a portal, and through the portal of the uterus, a woman can move to other worlds and other dimensions. Our uterus is a very smart organ as it has its own feelings, and this can affect us greatly. We all know that with the menstrual period our mood changes completely. I witnessed a caesarean section surgery many times and observed how a Gynecologist talked to the uterus after the baby was removed. It was amazing! The uterus contracted and the bleeding stopped from his soft, encouraging words of gratefulness.

This may all seem new and incomprehensible, but believe me, before each of us is an endless ocean of unknown. Go ahead, girls, be brave and explore.

Here is my story:

> *A gynaecologist saw one of my patients. The gynaecologist recommended that my patient cut her uterus out. The woman was seventy years old, and she had two adult sons, so she, without even thinking, agreed to the surgery. The day before the surgery, I met with her, and she asked me if she would be able to go to an English lesson in the morning (given the operation was at two in the afternoon). I advised her to stay home and chat with her uterus as it would be removed from her body in several hours. I also suggested, "Thank her for your two sons that you have, say goodbye, and ask forgiveness for your decision to have this surgery."*
> *Of course, this grandmother looked at me like I was crazy and said that she did not believe in this stupidity. As it happened, the surgery was complicated, and immediately after removing her uterus, this lady's heartbeat was 140 beats per minute. It was so irregular that she had to go through electroshock and she is now on blood-thinning medications for the rest of her life.*

Thus, you will understand from the above that I believe in the wisdom and deep interconnection of our organs.

2. BEHAVIOUR.

Behaviour is the cultivation of a strong character and feminine appeal. It is also the development of life skills, including the ability to listen, respect, have compassion, and be kind and willing. I love listening to lectures about how to read people's faces, how to react to provocative behaviour, or how not to offend people with my words. Good sources for studying these topics include modern psychologists and instructors. Listen to many but choose to listen to the advices that resonates with you the most. And always observe the behaviour of others and your own, too. Look for the hidden meaning of words and reactions. See the connection between the way a person speaks and how he/she behaves. This will save you from envious girlfriends, narcissistic and despotic guys, and unprofessional managers. Learn to control yourself in a state of stress. The older you get, the more obvious it will be for you to determine that the border between sincerity and bad manners, straightforwardness and tactlessness, duplicity and diplomacy is a fine and fragile line. You should learn to feel it in yourself and shape your own personality according to your own high standards.

I learned several things by listening to endless lectures on these topics. The first lesson I learned is that the paramount quality of our character is the ability to listen without interrupting, or without missing the information that a person is trying to convey. Dear Goddesses, if you like someone, show this person that you are honestly interested in his/her life. Light up your little star eyes, smile, be friendly, and do not condemn. It is not easy; I am still learning.

The second lesson I learned is that an outstanding quality is the ability to keep silent. In nine out of ten cases, keep silent, or at least think twice before saying something that you will regret in the future. Take some time out for a couple of minutes before lashing out with anger. These are mythical, fake victories, especially when we talk over someone. Verbal battles are not for true Goddesses. If your opinion or decision is critical, then make sure that the other side is ready to listen to you. Do not speak into the void as your time and message will be wasted. This means that you should not enter into verbal scandals at the provocation of your peers. In general, identification and controlling provocative behaviour of others is a scince. Take care of your nervous system and your energy by learning how to behave with maturity and respect.

The third lesson I have learned, and the habit that I cultivate in myself, is how to speak. Instead of "I" or "you", I use "we". We are so used to complaining about others that we don't see ourselves or our mistakes. The ability to see a team, a community, and a group of people united by common interests will create a pleasant and warm atmosphere around us. This is especially so if we say, "We can, we understand, we will achieve."

3. RELATIONS AND EXPRESSIONS OF FEELINGS–A SIMILAR TOPIC, BUT AT THE SAME TIME, A DEEPER ONE.

The people who surround us every day become a part of our life. First, these are parents with whom we often have a problematic relationship. After that comes a spouse, children, and friends.

How do we build these relationships? How do we choose our life companions?

Start asking yourself these questions and the universe will help you with the answers. My main advice is: **do not let strangers into your life too quickly and too close.** A girl is a delicious piece of cake in this crazy world. Truthfulness and naivete are impermissible luxuries, my beauties. Online dating, parties at unfamiliar places with strangers, romantic dates with unknown guys, and even drinks and food at strange places **are not as safe as what you would believe**.

God, these are all so dangerous. Do not do these things, my precious ones. I am sure that your relatives and teachers continuously tell you about this, too. Take care of your naiveness and truthfulness with all your strength. Be patient for the most durable, most intelligent person who will come into your life one day. That person will come, I promise you. Smile affectionately and they will immediately show you how strong their feelings are for you. And then it will hit you like thunder—this is the One! **Remember the golden rule: When your life partners truly love you, they will not share you with others, they will not insult you, they will not raise their hands at you, and of course, they will not force their will on you. Rather, they WILL PROTECT YOU.**

Have you seen a guy washing his first expensive car for half a day, then waxing it for another half-day while he blows the dust off it? This illustrates how much he cherishes his car. This is how much he will cherish the woman he loves.

4. LIFE SUCCESS, PROFESSIONAL SATISFACTION, AND CAREER

My dear girls, today the world needs real experts in their field as never before. One Greek philosophical treatise says, "Lord, do not bring me to live a life with an unloved person or to work on an unloved job." This means: Just do what you love. Find (or rather feel) what makes you happy and become the creator of your life. If you provide a creative attitude to your work and seek continuous self-improvement, everything else will come—prosperity, recognition, and respect. For love of one's work, plus creativity, plus knowledge equals faster career growth and professional success.

Remember sunshine, a Goddess CREATES, she does not do her job mediocrely (how many times do I hear – I do my job to pay my bills. I am so sorry for these people!). I believe in you. The universe believes in you. You are our only hope.

5. WEALTH AND FINANCIAL LITERACY

I admit that some girls will tell me now that men should take care of money and women should be in charge of the house. And this is right. Halfway. Because today, in almost all countries of the world, a woman lives a financially independent life, and a woman makes her financial decisions separately from her partner. This is worth striving for. Invest your money, learn to spend your money wisely, and improve your business education.

Always ask yourself questions such as: "How and where do I make money?"; "Where, when and what is profitable to buy?"; "How do I manage money properly?" etc. The first step is to learn how to NOT make impulsive purchases. Many people remain like blind kittens for their entire life when it comes to money. Very often, we see professors, doctors, and actors who are dying in poverty. My advice to you, my Goddesses, is: do not rely on a rich husband or the wealth that your family has today. **Count only on yourself**. Money loves order and self-respect. Listen to the lectures of the wealthiest people on the planet and cultivate their habits. Live according to your abilities. Be wise enough not to strangle your parents with endless demands to buy you more and more and more. Become rich, because you have achieved it for yourself. Let a worthy man come into your life who will take responsibility for your shared future. But don't turn into a lifelong little girl screaming, "I want this! I want that!"

Good luck, my Goddesses.

6. SPIRITUAL DEVELOPMENT

I read an interesting story when I was eleven years old. It went like this:

A rosy young apple fell from the tree. It landed next to a wrinkled, mature apple. Said the rosy apple to the mature one, "Look how young and beautiful I am. And you are old and wrinkled."
The old apple looked at the young one with love and answered, "The truth is on your side. And I wish you to get as old and wrinkly as I am, because then your seed will ripen from which a large and robust tree will grow."
But the young apple did not understand anything the old apple said and became offended.

Girls, even if you are beautiful at your young age (i.e. you are the ten in your physical beauty on a scale from one to ten), STILL- the most beautiful part of you **is your soul**. Your body will change over the years (bit by bit), but the infinite powers (the internal beauty) that the Lord has invested in you will continue to grow over the years and this will only become more and more beautiful. If you will invest in your internal world continuously.

I am a happy person. The Lord gave me an unusually exciting life with millions of opportunities, and thankfully, these were all the options that I wanted to choose from. I guarantee you, my precious ones, that there is nothing more disgusting than a stupid, harmful, empty, older person that has not made a single attempt to touch his own soul that the universe put into him at his birth, and who never took care of his spiritual development. I am talking about our spiritual and internal development, because this is a continuous process throughout our life, starting from a very young age.

Again, my Goddesses, I advise you to read the classics. Elena Blavatsky must be read all the time, throughout our lives. This woman led an incredible life and gave us so much learning in return. Her books explain The Great Evolution of our planet, Human existence, and Universal processes.

I also encourage you to talk with spiritually rich people and take an interest in the beautiful traditions of great nations. For example, in ancient Egypt, it was a custom to keep the pair of scissors that were used to cut the umbilical cord at a baby's birth. These scissors were then used a second time to cut the imaginary silver umbilical cord when this person died—symbolically letting their soul go into a new life. Isn't this enchanting?

Listen to the great Tchaikovsky, Mozart, and Beethoven. Admire the paintings of Aivazovsky, Van Gogh, Gustave Courbet, and Valentin Serov. Admire the sky, the sea, the stars. Admire the beauty of Mother Earth as there is no Planet B. Go to the theatres and collect everything that feels like inner beauty and harmony. Eternal happiness, spiritual growth, and self-satisfaction come from there.

7. ORDINARY LIFE CURIOSITY

This is a very commendable human quality. Curiosity develops a versatility of mental abilities, a unique attitude towards life, and the ability to see the barely noticeable opportunities that fate sends towards you. Thanks to curiosity, we develop observation, memory, and IQ levels. Ask yourself millions of questions about any situation, but most importantly, look for answers to your questions.

I remember when I was around one to two years old, that I could not yet speak. And yet, I remember thinking, when I will learn to talk, I will ask the adults how the spider makes so many thin, long webs. What kind of fantastic mechanism is hidden in its tummy that enables it to produce this web? Even today, many years later, I continue to ask myself hundreds of questions every day.

I also ask endless questions directly to my Creator. And **he always answers.** He helps me diagnose and treat my patients and sends me to the right places at the right time. Thanks to him, I have saved many lives while working in Israeli hospitals.

The Creator helps me understand and accept this world. For example, I recently asked the Creator, "My Loving Father, how do you want us to be spiritual like you if we are ordinary animals that are endlessly engaged in eating food, reproducing through pain, and suffering through sleep and disease? After all, we have no time and strength to be spiritual!" And do you know what he answered?

The creator said, "Do you remember Darwin and his theory that you descended from monkeys? Well, excuse me, but you are all still ape humans. The real spiritual people will come after you."

It was the Creator who hinted to me that you, girls, are who will become the real spiritual beings.

I also asked him the other day whether he is that true, pure, and boundless love, as everyone says him to be. And if that was so, then I asked him where does so much evil and aggression come from?

And he answered, "NO. I am not JUST THE LOVE. I AM THE LIGHT."

You see, the Lord is not just love. There is a lot of love and patience in him, but there is also anger and disappointment in him too, especially when we anger and disappoint him. The Lord is the LIGHT, the light of the sun that shines equally for everyone, regardless of who is rich and who is poor, who is beautiful and who is ugly, who is deserving and who is not.

This has a lot of inner meaning. It means that we have a right to get angry and to dislike. But we must also be bright and bestow this world with our light.

I urge you to speak with the Creator. Constantly ask him, WHY? And, for what? Don't give up until you find the answers to these questions. Tell him your thoughts and your fears, ask him for a blessing, tell him good morning and good night at the start and end of your day, and in all, doing so respectively. Simply talk to him and one day he will reply. You will hear him.

Let me remind you, my precious fireflies, that the purpose of my stories and in general this book, is not to teach you. You are all little geniuses who already have a head start in almost everything. Remember that I am writing this book to simply warn you against unnecessary mistakes and from any possible dangers that could distort or ruin your lives.

May the Lord protect you.

Truly yours,

Mama Nata.

NOTES AND REVELATIONS

5

THE RULE OF THE PICKLED CUCUMBER

We humans are social creatures; therefore, public attention and success are vital. I want to talk to you about the beneficial and detrimental effects of the environment on our lives. We will call this dialogue, "the rule of pickled cucumber." This is because if you put a fresh cucumber in a jar of pickles, after two weeks the fresh cucumber will turn into a pickle—just like all the other cucumbers in the jar. This is a very interesting experiment and I encourage you to try it yourself.

I discovered this law at the age of thirty. I accidentally found a book called, *Biology of Faith,* written by the great American scientist and biologist, Bruce Lipton. In his scientific experiments, he proved **that genetics do not affect our life and health as much as the environment does.** His book provides relevant material, and I strongly advise you to read (or listen to) all of his books. The meaning of his work is founded upon a huge amount of scientific research, and Bruce Lipton was able to prove that **genetics do not control our health.**

On the contrary, signals from outside such as the influence of the environment and the strength of our beliefs, influence the development and growth of our cells. Using a laboratory microscope, we can see how healthy cells die if we put them on a dish with diseased cells. Conversely, diseased cells recover if they are placed in a platter with healthy cells.

The meaning of this discovery completely turned my life upside down. As a nurse, I saw every day how seriously ill people were full of motivation and had a desire to fight for their lives as long as positive people surrounded them. That was until they went to the doctor who told them that their disease was incurable. Then, these patients all died within a few days. And there were many such cases.

What I will tell you, my beloved children, is that who you decide to become your friends, classmates, and teachers is a serious step in your life. This decision will require you to think and to feel your body and your energies while communicating with others. It is vital to choose people who develop your horizons, who dream and strive for the same things that you do. I speak with extraordinary girls whom I call "almighty Goddesses." In my soul, I assume that you too, my dear ones, also dream of your success, your abundance, and your achievements at a very young age. I imagine your faces, your beautiful eyes full of love, and your wonderful smiles. As such, your happiness and your success will also be my happiness and success. I will sincerely rejoice in your victories, I assure you.

So, by following the rule of the pickled cucumber, if your friends are not happy with your victories, if your happy eyes do not make them happy, then they are not your friends. Based on my own experience and those of the people around me, I sincerely believe that it is better to be alone than to try to adapt to stupid people who are not interested in me, even if they are rich and powerful. Generally, I respect loneliness. Loneliness is often a prerequisite for great insights and true understanding of oneself whereas copying other people's behaviour could harm your nature or destroy the inner harmony of your soul. As a result, this could lead to numerous diseases and mental disorders.

In an unhealthy environment, inappropriate friends will inhibit your development and block the flow of cosmic energy. Communicating with negative, constantly nagging people, will make us feel sick and broken. I have had such people in my life. They usually complain that no one understands them, they are easily offended, and they love to quarrel.

I once encountered such a person. He was a professor from Venezuela. He told me about his country and mentioned that there are a lot of beautiful women in his homeland. Indeed, there are a lot of beauty queens from Venezuela.

I replied with admiration, "How amazing your country is! Every second person is either a professor or a beauty queen!"

A couple of days later I ran across this man again. He was in a bad mood and was looking for a reason to release his negativity. He told me with a grimace on his face, "During our last meeting, you really offended me!"

"How?" I asked him in complete surprise.

He said, "You said that in Venezuela it is easy to become a professor or a beauty queen and that everything is bought there for the money."

I don't encourage you to go and prove to such negative people that the world consists of more than enemies and traitors. It is simply impossible!

This is just one small example of how difficult it is to interact with people who are not in unison with you. But how do you understand who is suitable and who is not? How can we distinguish a real girlfriend from an envious or gossipy one? How can we understand if the young man or woman that we like is capable of love and that their spiritual development is at the same level and direction as ours? Well, there are several strategies that you can use to understand this.

If the time that you are spending with people flies unnoticed, if you have talked to a person for half a day and you feel that it has only been a few minutes, then this is your person. If after the communication, your soul is calm, it feels clean, and there is no headache or feeling of fatigue or you do not want to go to sleep for a nap; then this is your person.

When communicating with "your" type of person, you do not have to make endless excuses, you will not be interrupted in mid-speech, and you will not be laughed at because of your clothes. You are not going to be asked too many inappropriate questions, and you will not feel like you are imprisoned at the police station. A person who is suitable for you will neither complain constantly nor judge your mutual acquaintances. He (or she) will be interesting, friendly, and polite to people around, and animals and kids will love him (or her) as well. He (or she) will enjoy insignificant and pleasant things that he (or she) may do for others. I may have just painted a portrait of those people who suit me, but the essence of this dialogue is to provide you with living examples that will help you to create your own habitat to become as healthy as possible so that your development will unfold as a beautiful rose in the garden after the rain.

Do not think that such people do not exist, because there are actually a lot of them in the world. I am writing these lines in Israel as I sit on the shore of the Mediterranean Sea. An old man just walked past. He paused, turned to me, and said, "I apologise. I can see that you enjoy the weather and the sun very much. Can I offer you a hot coffee? I live nearby; it will not be difficult to make you a cup of coffee." Immediately, daisies bloomed in my soul because I knew it was the Lord who had sent me a good soul to confirm the accuracy of my words.

To conclude our conversation, I just want to add something important: **Until there is a sincere desire in your heart to see others happy and successful, until you feel that doing good for others is a pleasure, you will not deserve or receive your perfect environment.**

My dear girls, great Goddesses, I am sure that you are our planetary generator of love, compassion, mercy, and creation. I do not doubt that you will all be incredibly happy and live a decent, beautiful life.

Please, choose your environment consciously and carefully.

It was a great pleasure to chat with you, precious girls. Be sure to read Bruce Lipton. He is incomparable. And by the way, I was lucky to have a chance to meet him in person. What an extraordinary soul! He signed my book in Russian. May the Lord protect this pure, good soul.

Goodbye, my beautiful Goddesses.

I will pray for you all,

Mama Nata.

NOTES AND REVELATIONS

6

THE LONG PATH TO YOURSELF

For millions of years, society has trained (there is no other word to describe this behaviour) young women for their significant future role as a male servant. Historically, generation after generation, women's lives have been decided for them from the moment of their birth. For example, in Arab countries, people used to say, "It is better to buy a bag of nuts than to have a daughter."

Girls of the eighteenth and nineteenth centuries were married according to the decision of their parents. It never occurred to them to make these decisions themselves. It was a blessing if a worthy man came into their lives, and their life proceeded according to the standard scheme—a husband, children, and the household. Women, until the middle of the last century, did not work, could not study, and did not have the right to vote in elections. And even today, in many Arab and African countries, a female's lot in life is merely terrible.

In this section, we will talk about how to attract a worthy partner into your life, or rather, how to choose the right one. As a rule, there are few great men in this world because they are not born that way, rather they become. I know you are asking, who makes them like that? We do. The girls! Napoleon, Peter the Great, Alexandre Macedonian, Picasso, Salvador Dali, and many others prove my point.

I understand that the world has changed, and preferences are different today. Some girls will like men and some women. I will not switch from gender to gender in the following passage, but the strategies I discuss in this chapter are more suited to heterosexual relationships. Skip it, dear princesses, if it is not for you.

Women are special and unique in the fact of God's purposes. And so, our development is critically important, not only for us and for our relatives, but also for the whole planet. Therefore, the sooner you begin to understand this, the sooner you will become a unique person, and the more significant results you will achieve and provide to this world, my precious ones.

If you are between ten and fourteen years old, and you do not want to think about these serious questions, then at least listen to what I have to say. When my grandmother saw that I did not understand her stories and instructions, she told me, "I know that you are still too young to understand me. Just remember that the time will come when you will understand everything. Just listen to me now because that time will come, and you will hear me."

As I have said many times and will continue to insist for many more, the true woman is a Goddess. All women are a powerful source of love and a source of many types of energy. Without women, this world will simply cease to exist given it feeds the people around us and the entire planet—potentially even the whole universe. A high level of goodwill, a level of inner nobleness, and the ability to have compassion are the leading parameters of a healthy and successful woman. My Goddesses, the deeper your connection is with nature and the brighter and deeper your desire to do good in this world, the more successful and desired you will become.

Are you asking, "Where do we get all this energy that we give to the world like little suns?" And, "Where do we get the power of love and kindness?"

Let me tell you.

Sources of energy

OUR CREATOR

The first source of energy, of course, is our Creator. And believe me, his strength is always with us. Talk to the Creator regularly. Ask him for blessings and advice. I do not know in what kind of families you are growing up, or how much he is discussed at home, but I assure you that without a constant internal dialogue with our Creator, we are like an iPhone without a battery. We won't last long. Please, let me be clear that I am not talking about churches or ceremonies or types of religion. I'm talking about close contact between the Creator and me, his daughter. And from this contact, I receive (as you will): energy, wisdom, intuition, and internal forces for victory and prosperity.

THE SUN

The next source of energy is the sun. The energy of the sun feeds plants and all living things on this planet. Imagine if one day, the sun disappears. It would be a complete disaster, right? So, enjoy the sun as much as you can. It is vital to look at the sun in the morning when it first rises, and in the evening when it sets. Look at it with open eyes but squinting a little. In those moments when you look at the sun, vitamin D will penetrate the cornea of your eye and the Sun energy will go straight to your blood where it will activate your hormonal and immune systems. The sensation of sunlight into your eyes should be comfortable.

BELOVED PEOPLE

Another source of energy, beautiful girls, is our beloved people. When giving them warmth and sending kindness, we receive even more warmth and goodness in response. The energy of love is a powerful stream that is similar to the Great Nile River. Additionally, when interacting with smaller children, we also receive a lot of good, positive energy. And, the more significant the difference is between our young friends and us, or even between our younger brothers and sisters and us, the better we feel after talking to them. Have you ever noticed how grandparents adore their grandchildren?

COMMUNICATION WITH PLANTS AND ANIMALS

The next source of energy is found from communicating with plants and animals. Believe my words, the kindest and the most humane people in the world are gardeners and veterinarians.

FIRE

The ultimate source of energy is fire. From the moment fire appeared on this planet, people have liked to sit around it and enjoy its warmth and light. On long winter evenings, I encourage you to enjoy the candlelight. Or, if you have a fireplace at home, then use the light from the fire. It is very calming and restoring.

Also, it is important that you try to find your own individual source of energy. The source could be from dancing, singing, drawing, yoga, or reading books. Find this outlet and enjoy this activity as often as possible.

Sources of energy are everywhere around us. Use them to recover, and cheer yourself up. You will feel that your body is lighter and that your soul is calmer and cleaner. You will want to live and enjoy life. These are sensations a person should be experiencing all their life! When you finally feel a tremendous, all-consuming love that is providing you with energy, then you will begin to understand what I'm talking about and why obtaining this energy source is so important. And remember, my precious ones, the pure energy of love does not require evaluation, gratitude, or even reciprocal feelings. All you need to do is fill yourself up on it and live your life by continually nourishing yourself.

You are small suns, tiny solar panels, and human fireflies bringing light, creation, prosperity, and hope into this world.

THE FIRST DATE

In this next section, I want to give you some tips on how to choose the right partner. I encourage diversity of choice and embrace all kinds of sexuality, but for the purpose of this chapter, I will refer to your chosen partner as a man. However, this reference is interchangeable.

Sometimes, it may seem like the guy is choosing us, my Goddesses, but this is not the case. We select our partners in life for whatever period that we want to be with this person. Therefore, I will give you some tips for your first date. Of course, we want this guy to like us, so we start to choose outfits and cosmetics, perfumes, handbags, and heels. And here is my first secret: **Men do not see the details; they see the big picture.** But most importantly, they will not look at our appearance (no matter how beautiful you are) but rather the energy that you carry in yourself.

Here, I refer to your level of goodwill, positiveness, and support (even if only verbal), that you bring to that first date. This is because boys are usually scared of a super-duper beautiful girl, so do not put the guy through hell on the first date; take pity on him and let him open his own goods for you first.

The first date is his, not yours. This is how it works in the animal kingdom and how it also works for us, as people. You must remember that you are going to choose a worthy partner and a noble friend for an indefinite period of time, or as long as you want. In this way, do not beg the guy for a relationship and do not try to make him like you by force. This simply does not work. **He** should be trying to please you. **He** should be trying to impress you. Not the other way around.

My other advice to you is to give the modest and shy guys a chance, too. Among tranquil people can be found a fascinating boy. A very handsome guy is cool to have, but remember, such a miracle could be "the property of the people." Devotion is not expected, and I am personally attracted to a man through his mental and emotional intelligence rather than his physical appearance. You must decide for yourself. What are you looking for? What do you need? And what do you like?

So, on the first date, simply emphasize the main points of your appearance. This is not a wedding party—yet. If you have gorgeous eyes, then add some beautiful cat-eye makeup, and if you have beautiful lips, then put on sensual lipstick. If your hair is amazing, then invest in a hairstyle, etc. There is no need to fight for him on the spot; it's too early. And later, this may be a big problem if you need to get rid of an unsuitable guy that is enchanted by your unearthly beauty. Additionally, if this guy is not what you need, you should think about some strategies on how to retreat so that you don't have to meet this person anymore. However, you need to do this in a way that does not offend him.

Now, let's talk about how to behave. We girls (mostly) prefer to listen and smile. If the man doesn't like to talk, then you will take the role of a leader. Usually, guys are talkative and love to talk about themselves. So, while letting him talk, observe him. Listen while assessing his level of sloppiness, his nails, his shoes, his smell, the condition of his teeth, and most importantly, feel with all your heart if he is your person. As a result, after five to ten minutes of conversation, you should have an idea if he is or isn't your person. If not, then politely prepare for a retreat. However, if he is what you need, then begin to charm him.

How do we understand if a guy is our man? If he is your man, then you will like the way he dresses. You will love that he is unobtrusive in his views, that he shares no vulgar jokes, he is an exciting communicator, and he is a gentleman (i.e. he does not assault you or try to grab you up like a drunk bum in the market). Think about all these things before you date him.

First of all, think about who you may want to be with and what may interest you in a boy. You do not go to the store to look at the products and then decide what you need, right? No. Because you already know exactly what you need to buy and what you lack at home. Choosing a partner should be done the same way. Try to understand the smallest details to determine what kind of boy might interest you.

I know your next question is: How do we charm the boy we like? **Start by talking about him**. All guys like it when girls talk about them. Most preferably, speak about him with inspiration and do not forget to praise him as much as possible. In general, a **boy should always be appreciated.** It is a golden rule because when we praise a boy, the level of his male hormones jumps to heaven and wings grow on his back. Remember, girls, that behind any great man is always a loving and beloved woman who inspired and supported him in the most challenging moments and believed in him like no others. I talk about a deeply loving woman that encourages and motivates her partner.

So, my Goddesses, praise him and give him a lot of compliments as well as a lot of humour and charming smiles. And if you managed to make your guy laugh on the first date, you will remain in his memory for his entire life. I encourage you to sincerely laugh at his jokes, even if they are not very funny. This also means the first date will be friendly, and time will fly by due to your skills and efforts.

Conversely, if you meet up with this boy for a second date, please try not to use the following phrases when communicating with your friend: "Where have you been?" or "Why didn't you call me?" Guys cannot stand it when a girl tries to control them or infringe upon their freedom. It is better to say, "I'm happy you came. I'm glad you called. I was looking forward to it."

If you have met the "One," how soon can you have a closer relationship with your chosen boy? My advice, my dear precious girls, is that boys are hunters by nature and blood, and subsequently, they hunt for their prey. Let him play, look for you, and dream about you at night. And during this time, you can determine your feelings about him. If you have used this time wisely, you will know if it is time to take the next step. If your guy is not ready to wait and he shamelessly rushes you to move into the next stage of your relationship, then this boy is not your person.

I will give you one more piece of advice: **Always disagree with the unhealthy habits of your chosen one**. I'm talking about everyday consumption of alcohol and drugs. Try to stop it. But if your boy came from a family that indulged in these every day, do not waste your precious time. He is not for you. Do not even try to like him or share a glass of vodka or even worse. To me, it seems that these days, the younger generation has lowered its behaviour to the point of sewer holes. Movies are crammed with scenes where young people drink like pigs, prick needles, smoke, and vomit in toilets. I do not believe that real life is this bad. I don't even believe that you, my girls, can behave like that or even want to. I'm left wondering who needs it? Who encourages our young generation to accept this behaviour as normal? NEVER DO IT PLEASE!

Imagine that you are walking along the street and accidentally step on dog faeces. How will you feel? Awakened disgust? Remember this feeling and attribute it to the inexcusable behaviour of others. So, if your boyfriend drags you into these types of activities (drugs, alcohol, etc.), do not love him! He is your enemy. This is not your soul mate.

I know for sure that the "One" will never share his woman with others. Rather, your partner will protect you as a theoretical future mother of his unborn children. Mother Nature put into him this vital instinct. Of course, that is if he grew up in a family where his mother was not beaten, humiliated, or insulted. It is crucial to understand what kind of family your boyfriend came from, and it's not at all embarrassing to ask what his parents do for a living or where his house is located in the city. All these details are as important as the person himself. Choosing a partner or friend is a serious business. Be attentive from the beginning of your relationships so that you do not become attached to a person who could ruin your life afterwards.

Choosing a friend should be very meaningful. Your soul, your reputation, and your body are invaluable gifts. Never forget it please.

I never had the fortune to speak heart to heart with an older woman when I was your age. As a result, I went through two divorces before I found a worthy partner in my fifties. I wish I'd been able to talk openly to someone who could explain all that I wanted to know. Still, I am grateful to God for saving me from endless short-term relationships, from humiliation, and from unworthy diseases. Therefore, I'm talking to you now, my smarties, my dolls, my precious Goddesses, and I'm telling you to love the worthy and become attached to those who deserve it. Be sincere and friendly, but at the same time, observant and selective.

It is in men's blood to make an impression, and it is important that we see his real face. Because if a boy genuinely loves you, he will always find time for you and will treat you with great care. He will make you comfortable and will always find a moment to communicate with you. **He will trust you.** And these are all essential qualities. So, my Goddesses, appreciate the boy who believes in you. Do not insult him with deceit and betrayal, or destroy his confidence in his relationship with you, because the boy will cease to trust you for the rest of his life. I beg you: Do not take sin into your soul; be honest with yourself and with the people you love.

The purpose of this conversation, my priceless Goddesses, is to protect you from life-threatening mistakes, from unwanted pregnancies, dirty diseases, humiliation, and tears on your pillow. And yes, all of this can come from one meeting and stay with you for life. Today, Western culture is far from the spiritual development of society. For some reason, we have low life standards, multiple and meaningless relationships, less and less respect and loyalty, and promises that do not last long. Conversely, I encourage you to take an interest in how young people live in India, Africa, and the Middle

East. Look to their cultural heritage and that of other nations. There is a lot to learn from them.

The future is yours, my girls. Do not be naive and do not commit irrational actions. Be conscious creators of your future. Let it be so.

Sincerely yours,

Mama Nata

NOTES AND REVELATIONS

7

GOOD MORNING, GOD. TODAY I BECAME A WOMAN

*D*ear and precious ones, if our previous conversations could be read by guys too, this section is just for us, for the Goddesses who want to understand their body in all its splendour.

A girl is born in the same way as a boy. In this I mean that the process of giving birth to a girl is no different than how boys come into this world. But the role of the girl is extraordinary, and her body is fraught with many surprises that appear gradually with age. These surprises change the girl's life 180 degrees.

One day you will find some blood between your legs. Please do not think that you are dying (as this is what I felt at the age of thirteen when I woke up and saw blood). This is called menstruation and it is a natural process that all women go through every month. I'll tell you why this happens every month and for how long a woman can have her period. I will also explain how to take care of your female organs. And, as always, I will convey this in a simple and understandable language, and whoever wants to know more can ALWAYS find additional information.

So, what is it, this menstruation?

To begin, let's look at a little anatomy lesson to better understand this topic.

In the middle of the lower abdomen, we have a brilliant organ called our uterus. The female womb is in a dormant state until the age of eleven to fourteen years (this is very individual). The uterus is like a crystal vase, both in its appearance and its fragility, and I am firmly convinced that all organs have their own mind. Therefore, I believe that the female uterus is a very wise organ. One day a baby will grow in it, and as such, the uterus will feed it, PROTECT IT, AND WARM it.

There are two tubular structures on either side of the uterus. Their task is to connect the uterus with two sacks (called the ovaries) in which the female eggs are stored. These cells are like chicken eggs but microscopic. From these cells, our future babies will develop. They begin as a new organism that will one day begin to grow and turn into a new person. This is a real miracle. I have worked in the maternity ward and seen childbirth many times. Intellectually, I understand how the fetus grows and what chemical processes are behind it, but every time I have witnessed a birth, I have stood there spellbound, hardly able to hold back tears as I witness this miracle.

I hope this is clear. Women were created by God (and mother nature) in the wisest way. Especially when you consider that for these eggs to enter the uterus and turn into a baby, many different cascading processes must occur, all of which are intimately interconnected with each other.

FEMALE HORMONES

Let's go back to our periods now. In addition to physiological and anatomical features, female hormones also play a crucial role in the menstrual period. It can be said that hormones are specific proteins that continuously communicate with each other. This communication is similar to the transmission of orders in the army. The General issues a rule, then the Colonel sends this order to the Major. The Major gives it to the Lieutenant and the Lieutenant to the soldiers. Outwardly, under a microscope, it looks like a salute for Independence Day—first a massive explosion of lights, then small lights appear from the large lights, and in the end, millions of sparks melt in the air. A similar process occurs with a girl's body every month. Isn't that wonderful? The primary hormone is released from the hormone centre in the brain. The following hormones (Majors and Lieutenants) separate from the female organs all by themselves (from sacs in the ovaries that are located on both sides of our uterus).

The most prominent female hormones deserve to be remembered by their names, and these are progesterone and estrogen.

Estrogen makes us feminine, gentle. It is responsible for the condition of our hair and skin, the size of our waist, and the quality of our bone tissue. Estrogen modifies female organs for adulthood. Progesterone is responsible for the growth of the mammary glands, and for the production of milk for a newborn.

Let's consider that these are two sisters, or rather, twins. One sister, estrogen, prepares the uterus for about three weeks to accommodate the baby. Estrogen tries to build a warm and soft bed inside the womb, consisting of blood vessels and millions of cells full of vitality. During this period, the level of estrogen in the blood is higher than progesterone. After these three to four weeks, if no egg is fertilized, progesterone says, "Listen, honey, you have built everything here, but this time there will be no baby. Let's clean everything up in here so that you can start working again next month." The level of estrogen in the blood falls, and progesterone levels rise. As a result, menstruation (or our period) begins.

During menstruation (which can last seven to fourteen days and is very individual), the girl bleeds from the vagina. Through this bleeding, the uterus is cleansed wholly from the inside and at the same time, so is the whole body. During this period, a woman usually feels weakness, loss of strength, apathy, and even a little sad. Menstruation is often accompanied by pain in the lower abdomen (known as cramps). This is because the uterus contracts and expands to cleanse itself.

And now, the important things to know are:

1. The first time your period starts, is again, very individual. Some girls may start theirs at eleven, and some at fifteen or even sixteen. And this does not mean that the sooner, the better, or vice versa, the later, the better. But it is essential to know that after a woman's first menstruation, she will stop growing. So, if a girl's period begins at age eleven, then she will remain the height which she was when her period started for the rest of her life. As a result, all tall and long-legged girls start to get their periods at sixteen to-seventeen years old. As a rule, a daughter will inherit this trait from her mother.

2. Menses (or the woman's menstruation cycle) are regular. Your period can start every twenty-four to twenty-eight days. And there are irregular ones too, especially at the beginning of menstruation. Having an experienced gynaecologist is essential throughout life. There is no need to run to an OB/GYN every week, but it is still worth knowing where their office is located.

3. At first, the amount of blood released from the body is small, especially that first time. But between eighteen to twenty-four years of age, the amount of blood lost during menstruation can be abundant and last between seven and ten days. This also suggests that the girl's body is ready to become a mother and raise a healthy and beautiful baby.

4. Pain during menstruation is very individual, from subtle to very strong. Remember that when sister estrogen is working, her sister progesterone is resting. In the language of physicians, the level of estrogen in the blood is high, and progesterone is low. And then vice versa, when progesterone grows in the blood, estrogen decreases. It looks like a pendulum swinging up-down, up-down. And the more significant the amplitude between these jumps, the sharper the pain felt during menstruation. This indicates that pain and bleeding tend to go in the same direction, as in the more it hurts, the more severe the bleeding.

Of course, menstruation is not fair to us girls! The good thing is that our period only lasts a few days. It is also why you, my beloved, are the real Goddesses. Our Lord created you as a priceless, crystal vessel in which one day a new life will grow. It may happen once, or it may repeat several times. Maybe the pregnancy will last nine months, or maybe seven or less. Or maybe the decision "not to be a mother" will occur. Well, no matter what occurs, respect your body as it accommodates a unique feminine part. Take care of it and cherish it.

It is fascinating to learn how great people of the past understood the state of health in general. The great Edgar Cayce (an American clairvoyant whose contribution in medicine and science cannot be overemphasized), advised that for us to be physically and mentally healthy we need to:

1. Serve the world and its people (!!!)

2. Be in constant contact with the ground: plant flowers, walk in the forest, live in a house, and attend to our garden, and

3. Have a healthy social life, a strong family, real friends, and a strong team connected with at least one favourite thing

Lobsang Rampa (a Tibetan monk and doctor), believed that to achieve good health, it is necessary to cultivate the main human qualities in ourselves, including truthfulness, purity of thoughts, asceticism, and mercy. Rampa also advised that we must fight the conditions that destroy our body and our soul, such as anger, fear, hostility, envy, hypocrisy, arrogance, and physical and mental carelessness as we talked about earlier.

In summary:

So, once again we have talked, my dear girls, about the importance and uniqueness of our bodies, and about the extraordinary ability of our body to cleanse itself. We have also talked about the exploding waves of female hormones that roll over us every month and how they completely reboot the entire body. We also talked about how the uterus is prepared for the opportunity for us to become mothers and then cleared of these preparations. We also talked above about the importance of protecting women's organs from inflammation and even mild colds. We discussed how long we may bleed - around one to one-and-a-half weeks each time.

I will not tell you about pregnancy right now, except that it is a profound and exciting topic. It is not relevant for you just yet, but know that pregnancy is a delightful time, making a girl uniquely beautiful and feminine.

Childbirth is not painful and scary. It is a natural event because mother nature created the process itself. The smell of a newly born baby is more beautiful than any of the most magical scents—more impressive than the scent of blooming roses, expensive perfumes, and even tastier than the smell of fresh coffee or a delicious cake. **The trick is to do everything in life, exclusively everything, with love and pleasure.** And, of course, to prepare for the significant role as a mother with great love and responsibility. This is because the more love and sincerity we put into this role, the more incredible the future generation of our planet will be.

Be eternally beautiful and feminine, my Goddesses. Let the people around you admire your beauty. Heal this world with your energy of goodness, light, and mercy. Fill the space around you with your unique scent: the scent of spring flowers, sea breezes, and mountain freshness. Intrigue, bewitch, and amaze the world with your knowledge and your unique vision of the beauty of this world. Create your soul and your beautiful body slowly, in deep thought and everyday work.

Take care of your body!

Protect your reputation!

Take care of your feminine purity and inviolability!

Let everyone around you walk half-naked and jump from guy to guy. All, but not you. Because you are Goddesses. You are the crown of our Lord's creation, his main pride and hope. I admire and love you girls. Remember how much I want your happiness. Remember how much I want to see you as kind and light.

Be happy!

Sincerely yours,

Mama Nata.

NOTES AND REVELATIONS

WOW, CORONA IS HERE!

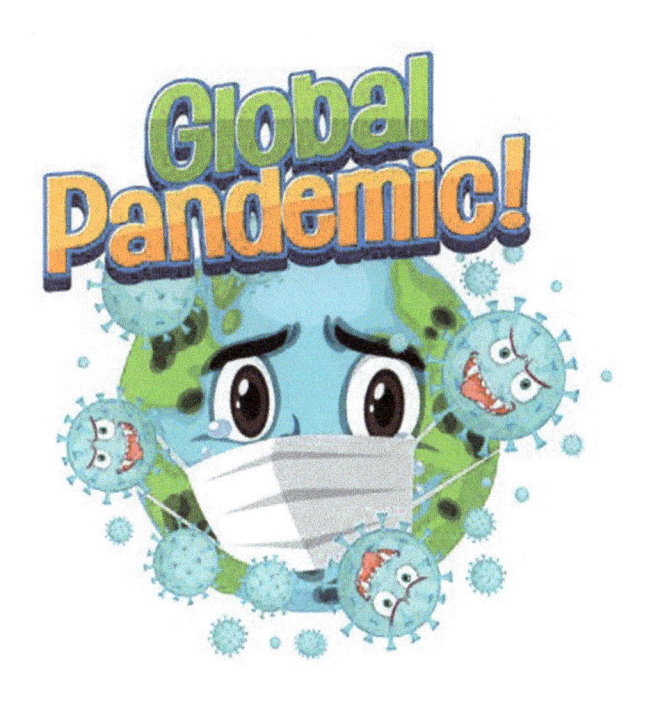

There is an ancient, funny Georgian story about Khanuma. Khanumas were women who in ancient times selected brides for grooms, and grooms for brides. These women, by the nature of their interesting profession, were very dodgy and knew how to "build their own business." So, the story goes that Khanuma once tried to sell a house on the bank of the Kura River. (Girls, look on the map. This river is in Georgia, a proud, small country located near the Caucasus Mountains.)

So, Khanuma praised her house and said, "If you want to drink water, here is the river, and here is your house. If you want to swim, here is your river and there is your house."

The buyer asked, "And what happens if there is a flood?"

Khanuma, without batting an eye, replied, "Eh, dear, where is the river? Where is your house?"

We all tend to see the same life situation in a broad variety of versions. Let's try to make a decision objectively so that everyone does not become emotional or stressed.

THE CORONAVIRUS.

Even though we haven't recovered from the Coronavirus, I have decided to talk to you about this topic, my priceless ones. The single reason why I wish to discuss this situation is that it offered an opportunity to show you how systemic stress may affect your life. To see the full picture, we will analyse this situation with the pandemic step by step.

Let's think about this calmly for a moment. Where is this Coronavirus? Is it here or overseas? Is it dangerous? Or is it a common viral disease? How do thousands of others get sick once a year for two to three days? My dear girls, the history of our planet knows many different, genuinely terrible epidemics. It has seen a smallpox epidemic, a leprosy epidemic, terrible diphtheria, the black plague, and the Spanish flu. If you do not know what I am referring to, there are many interesting movies and books about these events. As a rule, in real epidemics, the mortality rate is simply uncontrollable. Infection rates are like lightning, and the use of masks and gloves in such situations is, of course, entirely useless.

Characteristics of an epidemic include:

- The lightning speed of the spread.
- A high mortality rate despite doctors' efforts.
- The period from the start of infection to the peak of the disease is usually two to three days to deterioration.
- Response to treatment is slow or completely absent.
- After a full recovery, some permanent damage may stay with the person.

Now, compare these characteristics with today's situation and decide for yourself whether this epidemic is severe or not. Look around you carefully but turn off the TV and do not listen to propaganda (the news). My beautiful girls, in recent decades a lot of corrupt professions have appeared in this world, among them, first of all, in journalism. Therefore, you should rely on your own healthy logic and common sense. After all, you are spiritual beings, right?

So, the Coronavirus. What is it? A virus? An epidemic? A fatal disease? Who created it, and what is all this panic for? Who knows? No one will tell us for sure today. In my opinion, the best answers can be provided by Judith Mikovits, in her book, *Plague of Corruption*. This is a profoundly serious, facts-based book, and because of its content, Mikovits was arrested. But that is a different story, and we are here to talk about strategies that we can use to independently and objectively observe new life situations and not to panic with others. We must have our own independent opinions based on knowledge and internal wisdom.

I know for sure that an independent commission will be created in the coming years which will consist of smart and courageous people. They will investigate this whole situation, and those who deserve punishment will be punished.

So, given we are great Goddesses, we will now look at all the pros and cons of the coronavirus pandemic. First of all, we will discuss the pros.

1. Thanks to the Coronavirus, for six months there was not a single accident on the roads around the planet. People stayed at home and the pollution in the atmosphere dropped to almost zero.

2. Thanks to the Coronavirus, families finally became real. I'm talking about the fact that parents and children were given the most precious gift: the opportunity to be together, in no hurry. Finally, the children enjoyed their parents, and the parents enjoyed their children.

3. Thanks to the Coronavirus, we have all learned to save money, to cook, and to eat at home. We also had the opportunity to give ourselves the luxury of sleep and rest—maybe for the first time in decades!

4. Thanks to the Coronavirus, we finally thought seriously about what is essential in life and what is tinsel and what is vital to our health, as well as the peace of mind of our beloved people in the world. And all this is not expensive. Now, the biggest question is: Why do we work so much?

5. Thanks to the Coronavirus, unnecessary professions will probably disappear, but the essential ones will finally be appreciated. I am certainly not against singers and football players, but somehow, they don't make millions of dollars under lockdowns. However, we all need good ecologists and immunologists.

6. Thanks to the Coronavirus, many, perhaps for the first time in their lives, stopped trusting infinitely and said to themselves, "Enough! I will no longer be an obedient lamb!" People have truly appreciated themselves as SANE and ceased to be a naïve Pinocchio.

7. Thanks to the Coronavirus, I believe many have finally asked themselves the most important questions, such as: Why did I come into this world?

What is the meaning of my life? And how can I change this world for the better? I hope that these people got this great opportunity to be alone with themselves and think about this topic.

Conversely, what are the disadvantages of this ill-fated virus?

1. They say that many have died, but there are tens of hundreds of videos throughout the world showing empty hospitals. I myself, have been working this entire period, and all the hospitals in my state were empty. I believe that the numbers of sick, dying, or dead were most likely exaggerated.

2. A period of high unemployment has come, and this is not good. The Coronavirus is not to blame here but rather a lack of a professional approach to this situation.

Do you agree with me? What else can you think of? Somehow, nothing comes to mind.

I believe that what the Coronavirus did was scare people to death who had a lack of knowledge and a reluctance to think independently and objectively. Fear is a dangerous monster! Its grievous harm goes deep under the humans skin and paralyses us. It creates an ugly fantasy world in which there is no place for hope. And the less knowledgeable person who does not know how to acquire knowledge will have a higher level of fear in the blood. This state comes from the depths of our instincts, from a time when a person did not live but survived. From a time when they did not enjoy life but fought for a piece of bread; when they did not create but worked to stay alive.

So, don't you dare be afraid, my beautiful Goddesses! The worst thing that fear can create in our lives is stupid horror stories—an unreal world like in a movie. **Knowledge is a light of hope**. It is a culture of behaviour and the purity of thought. Knowledge brings development, calmness, constant improvement, and inner courage. Knowledge makes it possible to make the right decision in almost any hopeless situation.

Please forgive your relatives, my Goddesses, as they were afraid or are still scared. It comes from a great sense of parental responsibility that they bear for you, and most likely, their elderly parents.

Try to take control of the situation. You are our Goddesses! Go up to your mom or your dear father with a mirror in your hands and whisper in their ear, "My dearest, look here in the mirror. What kind of example are you setting for me?"

They will definitely come to their senses. They will not be offended; they will be grateful to you for the rest of your life. My son once told me so, and believe me, it was a one-time therapy! Since then, the invincible gladiator has lived inside me, forever and ever in the name of my sons! Girls, be merciful to your parents. It is not easy for them. Do not judge them! Pass them a helping hand in these difficult days and hug them once again. Praise them and thank them before going to bed. Consider writing a couple of kind words and leave a message for them on the table. Just one of your words or one of your smiles may mean that Coronavirus will no longer be frightening to them.

THE REAL CURE FOR ANY PANDEMIC

But still, how can we escape from viral diseases? From the Corona, from horns to hooves, and from various and other monsters? By wearing masks? No! By washing our hands every second? No! By dousing ourselves in alcohol until the skin on our hands turns into the parchment of ancient Egypt? Also, no! Who knows what to do, then? Of course, you do, my dear goddesses!

You are not journalists at CNN, chattering nonsense without a break. You are smart girls who know how to think independently, to carefully collect information, and to draw the right conclusions, all while relying on logic and your intuition (which by the way, never lets us down).

Of course, there is a need to continually improve the functioning of the immune system and cleanse the body of foreign invaders. Pay attention to what I just said: **We need to clean our inner world more than the outer environment.** This is because, for our immune system, viruses are without exception, common, natural invaders. For a healthy immune system, defeating any virus is like chewing on sunflower seeds or popcorn before bed.

And so again, let us talk about immunity and detoxing of the body. These two subjects are vital to talk about and are essential in an epidemic, including the Coronavirus.

A person is born without an immune system, and their first defence is given to them by their mother through her breast milk. After a few months, their immune system begins to grow. How exactly? Through these viruses that we sometimes get sick with! For the immune system, each virus is like a book that has already been read: **It is the knowledge.**

It is normal sometimes, to sneeze or get sick with a viral disease. Of course, there are hazardous viruses, and these are herpes viruses, hepatitis viruses, and the viruses found in cat faeces are especially dangerous to pregnant women. The Epstein-Barr virus (which is a different kind of virus that spreads by saliva through kissing and the sharing of drinks) is also rather severe. Still, having been ill with these viruses once, a person will forever have antibodies in their blood and will not be seriously ill with these infections again—provided their immune system is working correctly. What I am trying to say is that our immune system was created so wisely that it has the ability to self-heal and protect itself, and as a rule, the immune system almost always knows what to do.

What is it that kills our immune system, then? Primarily fear and stress. Now, do you understand why we have been intimidated? I would have been thrilled if with the same outcry, the whole world would have declared a planetary war on alcohol, cigarettes, and drugs because these are, indeed, our real enemies.

How can we improve our immune system?

1. By ingesting a lot of vitamin C. This can be found in oranges, lemons, grapefruits, kiwis, rosehips, amla, ginger, pomegranate, and spinach.

2. Being exposed to vitamin D, which comes from the sun

3. And of course, the right level of concentrated oxygen in our blood

Now, consider what we are being told. We are being told to walk in masks, which means that we do not have enough concentrated oxygen in the blood. We are being told not to go out, which deprives us of vitamin D. And we are being continuously told different horror stories and not a single kind word that gives us hope! Are there no sick people that have recovered from this "deadly" virus? Not a single one in six months? Really? It is in fact, the opposite! Thousands of people have recovered in two or three days without treatment! This is what President Trump wrote on Twitter after he was infected with Corona: "Don't be afraid of COVID. Do not let it dominate your life. We know."

So, my Goddesses, do some deep breathing exercises in the fresh air, enjoy the sun, eat vitamin C, vitamin A, vitamin E, and take zinc, silica, and magnesia. Be agile, run and jump, play, laugh, and enjoy life. For the more advanced, I would recommend taking a teaspoon of colloidal silver once or twice a day and some Noni juice. Also, Pau D'arco, chlorophyll, and catclaw as it is essential to take these natural supplements to prevent future viral diseases.

Again, I want to emphasize the importance of cleansing the body. I kindly encourage you to find the best detox program for yourself and use it once a week continuously. Refer yourself to natural herbs and plants that were created by nature itself—specifically those that have been used by our grandmothers and great-grandmothers for decades.

The following recipes protect the immune system. Please note that you should discuss the use of these natural remedies with your parents and your doctor first.

1. Lemon and Ginger Dressing – This recipe uses a one to one proportion. Wash the ginger and a whole lemon thoroughly. Without peeling the skin off, cut everything into small wedges and place into a small bowl. Cover the

ginger and lemon with honey and keep it in the refrigerator for twenty-four hours before serving. This dressing is delicious and an excellent cleanser that may be eaten two to three times a day, a few teaspoons at a time.

2. Turmeric - One of the most excellent anti-inflammatories and cleansing spices is from India, and its name is turmeric. It's a natural antiviral and antifungal remedy which I take as a spice by adding it to my meals. Some people like to take it as a pill.

3. Wormwood - The herb, wormwood, should be taken in a diluted solution (a cap of tea) at night, a couple of times a week. It has a peculiar taste, but believe me, it's better and healthier than chemical pills. I know of a clinic in Germany where doctors treat all types of diseases with wormwood. The only difference applied to the treatments is based on its concentration and in what way they administer it before meals or after meals, diluted as a tea, or just as dry grass.

4. Calamus Marsh - The medicinal plant, calamus marsh, can be used to cleanse the blood and intestines. Take it as a dry herb, a quarter teaspoon of this herb with water two to three times a week.

5. Bowel Cleansing - Proper bowel cleansing is crucial. Foods that help us cleanse the intestines include plums, tomato juice, walnuts, beetroot, and olive oil. You can also use activated charcoal or a little amount of hay tea. The most important thing to remember is that you should not have constipation.

If only all these remedies were touted on TV!

So, to come back to the point of this chapter, ask yourself, who wanted to benefit from the panic about the Coronavirus? Who wanted to turn us into obedient sheep? Time will tell.

Please understand that I respect all opinions and that these are my thoughts. But please know that all my advice is based on twenty years of experience that includes constant self-education, reading the great works of traditional medicine respected globally, and brave modern doctors who are not afraid to speak the truth.

Please remember, my beautiful Goddesses, that the essential mechanisms of the universe are:

Joy brings happiness.
Happiness brings luck.
Luck brings success.

Good luck always comes to people who know how to enjoy life. Therefore, I wish you joy and laughter, the courage to be yourself, and a healthy mind for a long and happy life.

Think about your health daily and independently. Stop the fear from the very beginning. Don't allow yourself to say, ''I don't know.'' Instead say, "I need time to gather as much information as possible on this issue in order to create my own opinion and find the right solution to this problem."

Health and peace to you.

Sincerely,

Mama Nata.

NOTES AND REVELATIONS

9

ALL THAT LOLA WANTS

*O*nce upon a time, there was a little girl. Well, not quite that little, maybe she was just in your age. She was a wonderful child. Inquisitive, cheerful, and kind.

One day she was having breakfast at the table with her family, which included her adult brother, her parents and grandparents, and her uncle who had recently come back from India. Everyone was talking about how to visualise their dreams. Uncle spoke with incomprehensible words about "meditation, chakra, vibration, cells, yoga, and asceticism."

The girl did not understand much, but she was very interested. All day she thought about what they were talking about. How could she become a wizard? How could she get rich quick? And how could she prevent herself from getting sick?

In the evening, the girl went to her warm bed, hugged her beloved bear, and fell asleep with that sweet sleep that only kind and bright children can sleep. That night, in a dream, the most important wizard in the entire universe came to her. He was the Great Creator himself, and he whispered these words into her ear, "I put you in the centre of the world to make it easier for you to observe everything that is in the world from the centre. I have made you neither heavenly nor earthly, neither mortal nor immortal, so that you, free and independent, could shape yourself into the image that you prefer."

And then the Mother of the Great Creator flew toward our girl (after all, everyone has a mother). The Creator's mother was very kind and bright, and she sang a very beautiful song to the girl. The words of this song were:

> *"Each reality is a choice of your heart*
> *Great choice changes in love*
> *Hearts dream and dreams are blown away by the winds*
> *Into the consciousness of unity, into the universal mind,*
> *Where gardens always bloom*
> *The hearts of the Gods create reality*
> *Filling it with the beauty of their love*
> *All the souls that dreamed are watching*
> *And hurrying to enter there*
> *Dream in love is always realized*
> *She plays and sings in her heart*
> *Like a bird, it rushes to the sky*
> *To find a new way of being*
> *Love is a joy and reason for everything*
> *And the bird of happiness visits those who*
> *multiply their beauty with their love*
> *and give their love for everyone."*

This song rushed from her lips like a mountain stream, murmuring in the girl's heart. It was imprinted on her little body, sealed in every cell. When the Mother of our Creator finished her singing, she laughed and said, "You can wish anything that you most desire. What do you wish for?"

And do you know what our girl answered?

She said, "I will ask you, the greatest of all mothers, to fulfil the most cherished desire of every living creature on our planet. But on one condition—that this desire will not destroy our world and those around us. On the contrary, it will bring light, harmony, and love to the world.

In the morning, the girl again saw her whole family assembled. Uncle continued with his reasoning about visualising dreams. The girl looked at everyone with a mysterious smile on her face and solemnly said, "I know how to visualize my dreams. And all your meditations, starvations, and cell vibrations have nothing to do with it." She told her family what happened to her last night.

A deathly silence reigned at the table. Everyone thought about the child's words and felt with all their hearts that the girl was right.

This is because visualization of our wishes requires two vital conditions, namely:

1. Our dream should bring light and kindness to the world.

2. We need to ask for blessings from the Creator for becoming our dreams our reality.

My dear girls, we have discussed how to choose the right environment for ourselves, and how important it is to be a spiritual and knowledgeable person. We've also discussed how important it is not to forget that we are above all, beautiful and unique WOMEN-GODDESSES. Please remember that I am not preaching to you in any way. You know a hundred times more than I do. The purpose of my communication, my precious ones, is based on an uncontrollable desire to convey how much we, adults, love you. You are very dear to us, and it hurts us that the world you came into is not as perfect as you deserve. But I am sure, and firmly convinced, that you will make it perfect. Through your uniqueness and inner and outer beauty, you will turn our land into a real paradise.

Yours sincerely,

Mama Nata

P.S. By the way, I strongly advise you to watch the movie, *Whatever Lola Wants*. It is a romantic drama directed by Nabil Ayouch in 2007, and I am sure that you will get great pleasure from it. Take my word for it.

NOTES AND REVELATIONS

ACKNOWLEDGMENTS

My bright and pure souls, my great Goddesses, all this time, I have spoken about the power of our Creator—especially his wisdom and the endless love that he has for us. Therefore, I dedicate my last lines to him. For the following, please assume that I am praying out loud and you are simply listening to me.

My great Creator, the only love of my life, I want to thank you for everything that you have done for me and continue to do. All my life, I continuously feel your presence, your protection, and support. Creator, do you remember when I was eighteen-years-old that when I gave birth to my first son, I never stopped repeating, "Heavenly Father! Holy Mother of God! Save me." Well, I gave birth to my son in less than a couple of hours without any pain or bleeding, and the doctors said that this does not happen, that I was cheating, and that this was not my first birth. I knew then that your bright blessing was with me.

Do you remember in 1996 when I asked you to help a woman in labour who was left without her kidneys after giving birth due to the fault of her doctors? Do you remember that only a kidney transplant could save her? She was told to wait for the transplantation of her kidneys for at least seven to ten years. Do you remember how I asked you to draw your attention to her grief? And on that same night, suddenly, a suitable kidney was found? The operation went smoothly, and the woman returned to a healthy, normal life, thanks to you, Dear Father.

Do you remember, God, how in 2000 I was preparing for my state exam to become a nurse? I was so afraid that my Hebrew would not be enough. Do you remember how I promised you that if you helped me to pass this exam, I would take care of my patients all my life like they were my family, just like my own mother or father or brother or child? At night, I dreamed of my children who said, "Mommy, don't be afraid of anything. You will pass this exam." And after that dream, I woke up and realised that our contract was signed for the life!

I'm trying very hard to keep my promise to you, my God, for you not only helped me to pass that exam but with your help, I have graduated from three universities and passed many exams under the most unusual conditions! Everywhere and in everything I have felt your presence, Lord.

You were always with me.

Do you remember when I worked in a hospital in 1997 as a nurse's assistant when the day of Kippur ended, and very little food was brought to the dining room? I went to the kitchen and made a scandal there, demanding exceptional food for the number of pregnant women who had gone hungry for twenty-four hours. Do you remember how I set the table and treated every believer there with respect and love? I asked you to do something beautiful for me, too. That night, you came to me in the image of an attractive man with sidelocks, and said to me, "You did something pleasant for my people, and I will do something enjoyable for you, too." And you, my Creator, gave me a date with my just deceased grandmother whom I loved very much. I had not been able to go to her funeral. It was a beautiful dream, Creator. Thank you for this dream.

Do you also remember, my beloved, how many times you guided me in my dreams, telling me how to treat my patients, and how to save their lives? Do you remember, my beloved, how many times you saved me from death when I fell asleep at the wheel from fatigue after yet another night shift? And remember, my God, how you came to me in a dream in 2013 and blessed me with a smile? You said, "I bless you." What did you bless me for? What did you mean by this? I am still trying to understand, my beloved Father!

I thank you, my Lord, that you let me see my sons, my family, and my friends just before the pandemic hit. You brought me back here, to America, on the last plane. For what, my only one, what are your plans?

My Creator, I ask you one last thing: Please protect and preserve our children! Do not let perverts and soullessness win the last battle of our planet! Illuminate this world with your light, your love, and your mercy. Bring your great power to our planet, in the name of our children and our future. Please, do it. Let it be so. Amen.

Girls, my dears, talk to him! Learn to read his signs carefully. They are everywhere, inside you, and around you. Do not miss these signs; be observant. If you do so, your life will turn into a fabulous conscious journey, equipped with a universal and most perfect GPS in which mistakes will be excluded. You will reach the primary goal of life. You will be a winner. You will be real Goddesses! God will help you, and I bless you too.

Men world is going through a complete fiasco. Enough of suffering, wars, and children's tears. Enough discriminatory attitudes towards women. We no longer want to see people who are hungry, sick, or unhappy, who are ruined by the system! Stop turning every living soul into a piece of biological meat that has been heartlessly minced by senseless rat races of suffering and vulgarity. It's time for the female future!

The time has come for a world in which all the colours of the rainbow will blossom. It will include rainbows of joy and success and peaceful coexistence in which everyone will live in complete harmony and interconnection. The universe, the human soul, and mother nature are all in this together. Everything will be one living, quivering organism.

Let it be so!

Truly so!

Amen!

Mama Nata.

AMULET

This is a powerful amulet, please cut internal part and put your picture inside. Now your book will protect you and bring you Universal energy. Be safe!

CPSIA information can be obtained
at www.ICGtesting.com
Printed in the USA
BVHW021312120421
604744BV00018B/480

9 781982 266578